100 THINGS TO DO IN MICHIGAN BEFORE YOU DIE

Friends Good Will, South Haven

100 THINGS TO DO IN MICHIGAN BEFORE YOU DIE

KATH USITALO

Reedy Press
PO Box 5131
St. Louis, MO 63139, USA
reedypress.com

Library of Congress Control Number: 2024949026

ISBN: 9781681065717

Design by Jill Halpin

Cover photo courtesy of Kath Usitalo.

Unless otherwise noted, all photos are courtesy of the author.

Printed in the United States of America
26 27 28 29   5 4 3 2

DEDICATION

Thanks, TJ, for all of
The Phunn Family Adventures

Guardian Building, Detroit

CONTENTS

• •

Music and Entertainment

Sports and Recreation

Culture and History

Shopping and Fashion

ACKNOWLEDGMENTS

Many thanks to the multiple people, resources, and tourism offices across the state that I've had the pleasure of working with throughout my career in promoting travel to Michigan and informing visitors about the wonders of the Great Lakes State.

Quincy Mine, Hancock

PREFACE

Greetings from the Great Lakes State!

Splashing in a salt-free sea and touring Michigan's two peninsulas are just a few of an infinite number of things to do in the Great Lakes State. Some are obvious, thanks in part to national media acclaim for our national parks, the indoor/outdoor attractions of The Henry Ford complex, the legacy of Motown, the comeback of Detroit, the rugged beauty of the Upper Peninsula, and car-free Mackinac Island. In the pages ahead, I also share lesser-known favorites of mine, discovered in a life of exploring and writing about Michigan.

You'll find references to popularly used terms in this one-of-a-kind, two-peninsula state:

- Lower Peninsula: LP
- Upper Peninsula: UP
- Mitten: Entire LP
- Mid-Mitten: Generally, the lake-to-lake belt with Lansing at the buckle
- Up North: Hotly debated, but generally City of Clare northward
- Thumb: City of Port Huron northward along the Lake Huron coast and westward
- Sunrise Side: Lake Huron shoreline from Saginaw northward

- Little Finger: Upper LP in the Traverse City region
- Tip of the Mitt: Petoskey and Alpena northward to the Straits of Mackinac

There's so much more to explore than I could include here. Please refer to several other books from Reedy Press about cities across the Lower Peninsula, as well as my books:

- *100 Things to Do in the Upper Peninsula Before You Die, 2nd edition*
- *100 Things to Do on Mackinac Island Before You Die, 2nd edition*
- *Secret Upper Peninsula: A Guide to the Weird, Wonderful, and Obscure*

Happy trails,
- Kath

Things you should know:

- Many Up North and UP businesses and attractions are seasonal—usually sometime in May to sometime in October.
- Bring cash; internet connectivity can fail in the UP and your card will do no good.
- The UP has one area code (906) but two time zones; it's mostly Eastern, but along the Wisconsin border there's a zigzag area on Central time.
- GPS in vast forested areas is unreliable. Pick up paper maps for go-to navigation.
- Find Pure Michigan visitor info and regional tourism resources at michigan.org.
- Stop at the state's 14 staffed welcome centers, located at key points along both peninsulas, for a wealth of free information and travel tips.
    - michigan.gov/mdot/travel/tourists/welcome-centers

The Copper Scoop, Calumet

FOOD AND DRINK

1

POLISH OFF PIEROGI
AT LEGS INN

Stanley Smolak had a dream, a vision, and the drive and talent to make them come true. The Polish immigrant worked in auto plants in Detroit and Chicago before finding his way to Cross Village in 1921. There, at a high spot overlooking Lake Michigan, he spent a couple decades building a fantastical structure of materials from the surrounding woods and water, as well as the local stove factory; Legs Inn gets its name from the hundreds of stove legs that define the roofline. The handcrafted building of trees, rocks, and stones is filled with Stanley's folk art sculptures. But it's not a museum.

Still in the Smolak family, this is a destination for good Polish food just like *Babcia* (Grandma) used to make. There are other menu options, but go for the golabki (cabbage roll), kielbasa (smoked sausage), pierogi (stuffed dumpling), potato pancakes, and szarlotka, a crumble cake baked with apples and mixed berries. And raise a glass of Polish beer or vodka to Stanley. Seasonal.

6425 N Lake Shore Dr., Cross Village, 231-526-2281
legsinn.com

2

SAVOR A TASTE OF HISTORY
AT EAGLE TAVERN

Mid-19th-century travelers would have stopped at the Eagle Tavern in Clinton, about 50 miles southwest of Detroit, for a meal and overnight stay en route to or from Chicago. The handsome white structure, built in 1831, was relocated to Dearborn's Greenfield Village, the outdoor living history museum that is a part of The Henry Ford complex. Eagle Tavern offers an immersive experience typical of dining in 1850, when the inn was run by Calvin Wood and his wife, Harriet. Servers are dressed in period clothing, and the menu reflects foods that were available locally in season. The summer bill of fare might feature fried tomatoes and peach pie, with butternut squash soup, pork fried with apples, and pumpkin pie in autumn.

The barkeep pours drinks of the era including hot apple cider spiked with rum, Pimm's cup, and whiskeys, as well as sarsaparilla and other temperance beverages. Unlike 1850, however, women are welcome in the barroom, previously reserved for the men. Eagle Tavern is open seasonally for lunch, and museum admission is required.

20900 Oakwood Blvd., Dearborn, 313-982-6001
thehenryford.org

3

BRING YOUR APPETITE
TO MEATS & MOOORE

Meats & Mooore (yes, three *o*'s) is a triple treat in Bay City: a butcher shop, the Mean Rooster Deli, and Meaty's Roadhouse BBQ & Sausage Shack, all under the management of Craig Owczarzak, a.k.a. "The Polish Butcher." His family has been a name on the local food scene for nearly 50 years; Craig and his two brothers grew up working at the store, which he ended up buying from their parents. He's usually behind the looong glass case selling quality meats; house-made Polish sausage; a variety of brats, fresh pastrami, and corned beef; and prepared foods (try the plus-sized meatballs). Craig expanded the operation to include the two dining options, with the Roadhouse open seasonally in a "shack" outdoors and the year-round deli in the same spacious room as the meat counter. Bring your appetite for one of the sampler platters—the Ultimate includes fall-off-the-bone ribs, barbecue chicken, brisket, sausages, and a choice of sides.

1411 S Wenona St., Bay City, 989-893-5413
facebook.com/MeatsandMooore

TIP

The Meats & Mooore building has a connection to Annie Edson Taylor, a Bay City schoolteacher who was the first person to survive a trip over Niagara Falls in a barrel. Murals tell the story of the structure's history as the West Bay Cooperage company, maker of barrels including the custom-designed craft that carried Annie over the cascades in 1901.

4

EAT PIE, LOVE LIFE
AT SWEETIE-LICIOUS

Linda Hundt is "changing the world one pie at a time" at her retro-cute bakery and café in the heart of a village that dates to the 1830s. The shop's red-and-white-striped awning hints at the vintage vibe inside, where Sweetie-licious bakers are in full view measuring, mixing, rolling, and handcrafting pies with high-sided crusts to hold mountains of fresh fruit, like the award-winning Tom's Cheery Cherry Berry. Pies, cookies, brownies, cupcakes, and muffins are displayed, like edible works of art, in pink paper-lined glass cases. Nostalgia is in the air, from the aroma of treasured old recipes (with a modern twist) to displays of kitchen collectibles like cookie tins and sifters, a child's toy oven here, a bright red clock radio there, and a 70-year-old Frigidaire stocked with cold beverages. Walls are lined with awards, accolades, and articles about the business that Linda launched from her home kitchen in 2002.

108 N Bridge St., DeWitt, 517-669-9300
sweetie-licious.com

FIND A SLICE OF PIE HEAVEN AT THESE BAKERIES AND CAFÉS AROUND THE STATE

The Cherry Hut

More than a century of making homemade cherry pies that started with a roadside stand. Seasonal.

211 N Michigan Ave. (US-31), Beulah, 231-882-4431
cherryhut.com

Crane's Pie Pantry Restaurant & Winery

Can't decide which pie to try? Choose the flight of four.

6054 124th Ave. (M-89), Fennville, 269-561-2297
cranespiepantry.com

Grand Traverse Pie Company

Cherries, the hometown fruit, star in many of the four dozen pies.

525 W Front St., Traverse City, 231-922-7437
Nine additional locations in Michigan.
gtpie.com

Peace Pie Company

Salted maple thyme, strawberry rhubarb—just a couple of the pies to bring you peace.

1501 Division St., Marquette, 906-458-6106
peacepiecompany.com

Sister Pie

Drool over inventive combos like lemony strawberry or blueberry plum balsamic.

8066 Kercheval, Detroit, 313-447-5550
sisterpie.com

5

ORDER WHITEFISH
WITH A LOCK VIEW IN THE SOO

Whitefish are native to the cold Great Lakes waters, and for centuries they have been an important part of the culture and sustenance of the region's Anishinabek people. In 1695, European explorer Antoine de la Mothe Cadillac delightedly noted, "Moreover, better fish can not be eaten, and they are bathed and nourished in the purest water." Long before "eat local" became a foodie trend, whitefish was a staple across the UP. Cooks have a field day with the mild and versatile fish, and it's found battered and fried, smoked, baked, and broiled, and in sausage, dips, and spreads. Goetz's Lockview Restaurant, a Sault Ste. Marie landmark since 1945, starts the day serving whitefish with eggs and bagels, and offers a choice of six ways with the fillet at lunch and dinner. Find it in chowder, tacos, a Reuben sandwich, and deep fried on a bun. You'll be hooked on the smoked whitefish spread made with horseradish, capers, and cream cheese. All that and a view of the Soo Locks, too.

329 W Portage Ave., Sault Ste. Marie, 906-632-2772
thelockviewrestaurant.net

TIP

For the best of the Copper Country, search "Keweenaw Whitefish Trail" at visitkeweenaw.com.

A FEW HIGHLIGHTS IN THE EASTERN UP

Gustafson's Smoked Fish

Picnic-ready fish smoked on-site, sausages, and dip.

W4467 US-2, Brevort, 906-292-5424
facebook.com/gustafsonssmokedfish

Moofinfries

Locally caught fish, fresh-cut fries, grass-fed beef burgers.

W11623 US-2, Naubinway, 906-477-9000
facebook.com/moofinfries

FOR A TASTE OF WHITEFISH IN THE LP

Hack-Ma-Tack Inn & Restaurant

Whitefish almondine is a signature dish at the historic lodge on Mullett Lake.

8131 Beebe Rd., Cheboygan, 231-625-2919
hackmatackinn.com

Jolly Pumpkin

Smoked whitefish dip so good, it could be dinner. Pair with a house brew.

13512 Peninsula Dr., Traverse City, 231-223-4333
jollypumpkin.com

Legs Inn

Start with a chunk of smoked whitefish and crackers or whitefish avocado toast.

6425 N Lake Shore Dr., Cross Village, 231-526-2281
legsinn.com

6

DRINK IN
THE CRAFT BEVERAGE SCENE

There's no shortage of craft beverage makers in the Great Lakes State. It's tough to keep up with the number of brewers, distillers, cideries, and wineries from Detroit to Copper Harbor.

The Michigan Brewers Guild counts 400 breweries, microbreweries, and brewpubs, ranking the state as sixth in the nation for craft beer. Nicknamed Beer City USA, Grand Rapids alone has more than 40 stops on its Ale Trail.

Michigan Wine Country lists events and dozens of wineries along seven wine trails in five regions across both the LP and the UP. The total number of wineries is about 200.

Hard cider, too, is growing in popularity, with about 90 makers.

Craft distilleries are booming, placing fifth in the US with about 90 makers of vodka, gin, rum, whiskey, liqueurs, brandy, and bourbon.

Michigan's tourism and agricultural industries benefit from the boom, so not only can you enjoy your beverage of choice, you can feel good about helping the state's economy.

Michigan Brewers Guild
Map of member breweries, info on four annual Beer Fests.
mibeer.com

Michigan Wine Country
Links to seven wine trails, wine event calendar.
michiganwinecountry.com

Michigan Craft Beverage Council
Maps and listings of the variety of craft beverage makers and events.
michigancraftbeverage.com/drink/trails-maps

7

SAY CHEESE
IN PINCONNING

There's a semihard cheese that resembles cheddar or Colby but has a personality of its own. Pinconning cheese is named for the town in Michigan dairy country where it was created in 1915 by cheesemaker Dan Horn to use up excess whole milk. It was his daughter Inez and her husband, Lawrence Wilson, who launched Wilson's Cheese Shoppe in 1939 and started marketing the mild, versatile cheese that can be eaten now or later. Pinconning becomes sharper as it ages (up to 120 months), and it is used in cooking, is snacked on with crackers or fruit, and is a natural on a charcuterie board. Fresh Pinconning is made into squeaky cheese curds and also makes a tasty cheese spread. There are two landmark shops that sell the iconic local food and other Michigan food products, both owned and operated by members of the local Saha family. Wilson's Cheese Shoppe declares its title of the oldest cheese store in the state, and the roots of Pinconning Cheese Co. go back to 1948. Look for the giant mouse mascot at both stores.

Pinconning Cheese Co. & Fudge Shoppe
221 N Mable St. (M-13), Pinconning, 989-879-2281
pinconningcheese.com

Wilson's Cheese Shoppe
130 N Mable St. (M-13), Pinconning, 989-879-2002
wilsoncheese.com

8

COZY UP
TO THE WHITEHOUSE

The neon "Open Hamburgers" sign that juts out from the Whitehouse restaurant is comically outsized for the building, the better for you to spot the tiny diner on the mid-Mitten City of Clare's main street. If you time it right, you'll be able to nab one of the six well-worn, cushion-free wooden booths without having to wait outside in the elements for one to open up—there's no standing-around space inside the snug spot. When two brothers opened the eatery in 1935, there were just three tables and specialties of the house were hot dogs and burgers. Today's expanded menu challenges the cook, just feet from diners, to juggle pancakes, eggs, hash browns, bacon, sandwiches, and burgers on the large, seasoned flattop. And the results are outstanding. Expect to be drawn into conversation with the friendly folks at the other tables—it's that cozy of a spot.

613 N McEwan St., Clare, 989-386-9551
facebook.com/openhamburgersclaremichigan

9

MAKE YOUR HEART GO FLIPPITY-FLOP

AT WESTON'S KEWPEE SANDWICH SHOP

Among Michigan's culinary claims to fame is the olive burger, created in 1923 in Flint at Kewpee Hotel Hamburgs. The early fast food chain was identified by the Kewpie doll and the ditty "Hamburg Pickle on Top! Makes Your Heart Go Flippity-Flop!" Its special sandwich was not a patty formed of olives but a juicy beef burger topped with loose, sliced green olives. Two years later, at the Kewpee Hamburg joint in Mid-Michigan's Lansing, the matriarch of the family business incorporated olives in a mayonnaise-based sauce and declared its version of the olive burger. Gladys Bowlin's secret recipe is still used by her great-granddaughter Autumn Weston, the fourth generation running Weston's Kewpee Sandwich Shop. The creamy, briny sauce tops burgers of certified Angus beef that are freshly ground daily and cooked to order in an open kitchen. Other burgers, sandwiches, and wraps satisfy those not in love with olives. Open weekdays only.

118 S Washington Sq., Lansing, 517-482-8049
westonskewpee.com

10

CROW ABOUT
CHICKEN IN THE ROUGH

Fans of fried chicken dinners have a choice of winners in the Mitten. Best known are two rambling restaurants in Frankenmuth, "Michigan's Little Bavaria," which was founded in 1845 by German missionaries. Both the Bavarian Inn, where servers wear dirndls or lederhosen, and the Colonial America–themed Zehnder's accommodate more than 1,000 guests at a time.

If you don't need the crowds or costumes, head to Port Huron and the Palms Krystal Bar & Grill for a great chicken dinner with more *ooh* and *ahh* than *oom-pah-pah*. The diner is the last in the US of the Chicken in the Rough chain, which launched in 1936 and once numbered 250 franchised restaurants. The light-and-crispy, broasted-style fried chicken is served simply with shoestring potatoes, coleslaw, a roll, and honey. It's a delicious step back in time; the art deco bar opened in 1936, and the main dining room has the feel of a 1950s diner.

Bavarian Inn Restaurant
713 S Main St., Frankenmuth, 800-228-2742
bavarianinn.com

Palms Krystal Bar & Grill
1535 Pine Grove Ave., Port Huron, 810-985-9838
palmskrystal.com

Zehnder's of Frankenmuth
730 S Main St., Frankenmuth, 844-207-7309
zehnders.com

MORE CHICKEN TO CROW ABOUT

Dam Site Inn

Pan-fried chicken with homemade noodles and biscuits and a retro supper club vibe with original Saarinen furnishings in the cocktail lounge. Seasonal.

6705 Woodland Rd., Brutus, 231-539-8851
damsiteinn.com

Iva's Chicken Dinners

The fourth generation is making the cast-iron fried chicken that Iva Ousterhout served at the boarding house she opened in 1938. Save room for the homemade pie. Seasonal.

201 Chestnut St., Sterling, 989-654-3552
ivaschickendinners.com

The Southerner

A taste of Appalachia in family recipes; try Nana's Table with fried chicken, catfish, biscuits, and a choice of sides including braised greens, grits, and cabbage slaw.

880 Holland St., Saugatuck, 269-857-3555
thesouthernermi.com

PICNIC
WITH A PASTY

If anyone needed comfort food, it was the UP iron and copper miners who headed deep into the earth every day to do hard labor in the cold and dark. The pasty (pronounced PASS-tee) filled the bill. The handheld pie of root vegetables and meat wrapped in a sturdy but flaky crust was introduced to Copper Country by Cornish miners and adopted by the Finnish population. Although the mining jobs dried up decades ago, the pasty thrives as a staple of the UP diet, and it is found at restaurants, bars, bakeries, and roadside stands. Unlike those miners, you can enjoy your pasty in the fresh air, at a picnic table, or at the beach.

There are fierce debates about who makes the best pasty and whether to top them with ketchup or gravy. (Hint: ketchup.) While the traditional combination of beef, potatoes, onions, and rutabaga and/or carrots prevails, it's increasingly sharing menu space with vegetarian, chicken, cheesy, breakfast, and dessert varieties. Pasties have even found their way to the LP.

So, who makes the best pasty? You be the judge. While the basic ingredients may remain the same, the results vary depending on the type of meat, the ratio to veggies and whether they're sliced or diced, the amount of seasoning, and the magic of the crust. Here are some favorites (in addition to those in the companion book *100 Things to Do in the Upper Peninsula*).

Upper Peninsula

Jolly Inn

8019 M-77, Germfask, 906-586-3334

Lawry's Pasty Shop Ishpeming

2381 US-41, Ishpeming, 906-485-5589

Lawry's Pasty Shop Marquette

2164 US-41, Marquette, 906-226-5040
lawryspasties.com

The Northwood Restaurant & Bar

29944 E Channel Rd., Drummond Island, 906-493-5282
northwooddrummondisland.com

For more, follow the Keweenaw Pasty Trail found at visitkeweenaw.com.

Lower Peninsula

Cousin Jenny's Cornish Pasties

222 E State St., Ste. 102, Traverse City, 231-941-7821
cousinjennyspasties.com

Barb's Pizza and Pasties

610 S Main St., Clawson, 248-797-5096
barbspizzaandpasties.com

12

SCREAM FOR
HOMEMADE ICE CREAM

Moomers, which started as a small ice cream shop next to a dairy farm in Traverse City, has scooped up national recognition and a place on northern Michigan to-do lists. *Good Morning America* and *USA Today* voters have declared Moomers Homemade Ice Cream the best, and the lines outside the door confirm its goodness. The family-run business makes more than 150 ice cream flavors and features at least 20 of them each day. The signature scoop is Cherries Moobilee (black sweet cherries, chocolate fudge swirl, and chunks of brownies), just one of 10 or so flavors that feature the locally grown fruit. Its Cherry Traffic Jam was once named the official hard-packed ice cream of the National Cherry Festival in Traverse City. Can't decide? Choose the ice cream flight for a sampling of five flavors. Got a gang? Go for the Wholey Cow: 10 scoops topped with multiple toppings, bananas, and brownies, served with a can of whipped cream.

7263 N Long Lake Rd., Traverse City, 231-941-4122
moomers.com

A SAMPLING OF MICHIGAN-MADE ICE CREAM HANDCRAFTED WITH CARE

The Copper Scoop

Locally sourced ingredients go into the small batches of ice cream and sorbet made on-site. Opt for the thimbleberry when the limited supply is available!

324 5th St., Calumet
Search Facebook for Copper Scoop Ice Cream

Hill Top Soda Shoppe

Signature ice cream flavors feature house-made chocolate chips and pecans sautéed in butter; sorbets are made with local fruit.

7117 South St., Benzonia, 231-882-9697
hilltopsodashoppe.com

Love's Ice Cream & Chocolate

Organic ingredients and grass-fed dairy from local farms make the difference at this ice cream shop found at the Grand Rapids Downtown Market.

435 Ionia Ave. SW, Stall 106, Grand Rapids, 616-965-1054
lovesicecream.com

MSU Dairy Store

Beloved Michigan State University campus tradition for exclusive college-themed scoops like Spartan Swirl and Buckeye Blitz made at the College of Agriculture and Natural Resources Dairy Plant.

474 S Shaw Ln., Room 1140, East Lansing, 517-353-3312
msudairystore.com

13

GET THE DWI
AT COPS & DOUGHNUTS

It sounds like a gag: "A cop walks into a doughnut shop . . ." But in Clare, the punch line is no joke. In 2009, when the city's bakery was on the verge of closing, the nine-member Clare Police Department decided to rescue the sweet spot, a main street fixture since 1896. Without an ounce of baking know-how, a dash of business experience, and a heavy sprinkling of good humor, the team managed to turn the cliché of cops loving doughnuts into a successful venture that attracts visitors from around the globe. It helps that the scratch-made baked goods are worth the drive and the atmosphere is fun but respectful of law enforcement, with merchandise like "DWI: Doughnuts Were Involved" T-shirts and bags of Morning Shift and decaf Off-Duty Cops Coffee. The mini museum displays patches from police departments across the country and police-related memorabilia, with a jail cell door for mug shots. Check the website for Cops & Doughnuts satellite locations elsewhere in the Mitten, called "precincts" and "sub-stations."

521 N McEwan St., Clare, 989-386-2241
copsdoughnuts.com

14

TASTE HEAVEN
AT THE JAMPOT

It was the early 1980s and Father Basil and Father Nicholas were in a jam. They'd been called to establish a monastery at a remote spot in the Keweenaw Peninsula but had no means of supporting it—until they learned to turn the bounty of wild berries around them into fruit spreads. Since selling their first jar of preserves in 1986, Poorrock Abbey has blossomed into a line of wild raspberry, blueberry, and thimbleberry jams, apple butter, plum rum conserves, and more. Their cozy Jampot shop, next to Jacob Creek Falls, draws crowds who line up for brownies, cookies, muffins, and other goodies freshly baked by the good-humored, bearded, cloaked monks. The Jampot is open from spring through mid-October; check their website for days. An online shop sells preserves, candies, and rum-soaked fruitcakes. The onion-domed Holy Transfiguration Skete and cloistered grounds across the road, on the shore of Lake Superior, are not open to the public, but visitors are welcome at the monastic gardens and on the woodland walking trails.

6500 M-26, Eagle Harbor
poorrockabbey.com

15

BITE INTO A BRAT
AT NOWICKI'S

You gotta love a place that made a sausage 8,773 feet long in a bid to secure the Guinness World Record in 1979. And it was reportedly delicious. There's still a whole lot of sausage stuffing going on at Nowicki's Sausage Shoppe in Alpena, on the Sunrise Side. Housed in a stately, turn-of-the-century, former German social hall, Nowicki's is a maker of some 80 food products, including German and Polish meats from five generations of recipes. The family-owned business is committed to using select meats and fresh spices—no fillers or preservatives. The tasty potato brat, for example, is 25 percent potato and 75 percent lean pork. The wide variety of brat flavors includes Russian Reuben, Buffalo chicken, Philly cheesesteak, and Michigan honey BBQ. They're available by six-pack and at lunchtime brat bars, offering a choice of six brats and multiple toppings served on a bun in Alpena and shops in Gaylord and Rogers City. Be sure to have the gigantic dill pickle, too.

1224 N 2nd Ave., Alpena, 989-354-2219
nowickissausage.com

625 W Main St., Gaylord, 989-448-2352

107 S 3rd St., Rogers City, 989-734-4100

PUT A DENT
IN A DETROIT-STYLE PIZZA

Detroit-style pizza is rolling out across the US, but the Motor City is the only place to try the true Sicilian-inspired pie. Gus Guerra introduced it in 1946 at his tavern, Buddy's Rendezvous Pizzeria. Baked in rectangular, high-sided, steel auto plant trays, the dough is stretched to fit the pan, and layering of ingredients shifts into reverse: first pepperoni, then Wisconsin brick cheese topped with stripes of red sauce. The specially proofed crust rises to a thick but airy consistency resulting in a crispy bottom with caramelized, crunchy edges. In 1953, Gus opened Cloverleaf Bar in a Detroit suburb, and in 1977, former Buddy's employee Louis Tourtois gave it his imprint at his Loui's Pizza. While Buddy's and Cloverleaf have multiple locations across Metro Detroit, Loui's is one of a kind, with red booths and straw-covered Chianti bottles, emptied and signed by patrons, dangling everywhere. Still a family biz, the pizza continues to rack up awards, and the antipasto salad is a must. Louis learned well.

Buddy's
17125 Conant St., Detroit, 313-892-9001
buddyspizza.com

Loui's Pizza
23141 Dequindre Rd., Hazel Park, 248-547-1711
facebook.com/louispizza

17

GO THE EXTRA MILES FOR SWEET TREATS
AT THE COOKIE CAMPER

Most mornings from spring through late fall, along a two-lane blacktop near Lake Superior, Ellen Airgood heads to the 1974 Argosy trailer, puts the coffee on, and sets out an assortment of freshly baked goods from recipes she's perfected over the decades. While this venture is just a few years old, for two dozen years she and her husband, Rick Guth, ran the popular Grand Marais West Bay Diner in a 1949 Paramount Road King that the couple restored.

After dishing more from-scratch omelets, pizzas, and cookies than they could ever count, they parked the "cookie camper" on their property near Muskallonge Lake State Park and named it the Uglyfish Baking Co. The focus is on Ellen's mouthwatering treats, from pie bars and crumble-topped muffins to cinnamon rolls and jumbo cookies. The unlikely name for the beautiful bounty is an interpretation of *muskallonge*, the Ojibwa word for "ugly fish."

Ellen is also the author of four novels including *Tin Camp Road* and *South of Superior*, recognized as Michigan notable books.

29357 CR-407, Newberry
facebook.com/uglyfishbakery

FEEL SUPER, EAT BLUEBERRIES

Michigan is in the top tier of blueberry-growing states, producing 90 million pounds of the tasty superfood. Commercial growing began in the early 1900s, and the state is a leader in highbush varieties. Wild blueberries grow well in both the LP and the UP, and long before they became an industry, Native Americans knew the nutritional and medicinal value of the berries without naming that goodness antioxidants, vitamin C, or manganese. Plucking the blue orbs at U-pick farms or foraging in the wild are popular pastimes in a season that stretches from July to September. Several festivals celebrate both the domestic and the wild kind, with blueberry food and beverages, pie-eating contests, and traditional festival fun. Although most blueberry growers and U-pick farms are located in southwest Michigan, there are a handful in the UP including Pancho's, tucked away in the Keweenaw Peninsula and found by word of mouth and hand-painted directional signs. See the Michigan Farm Fun guide for resources elsewhere in the state.

National Blueberry Festival
South Haven in August
blueberryfestival.com

Wild Blueberry Festival
Paradise in August
wildblueberryfestival.org

Pancho's Wild Blueberries
Highbush and wild blueberries, U-pick or they pick
34349 Big Traverse Rd., Lake Linden, 906-296-4561

Michigan Farm Fun Guide
michiganfarmfun.com

19

SNAP TO IT,
EAT A CONEY DOG

As humble as it may appear, there is an art to Michigan's special treatment of hot dogs, called Coney Islands. Introduced in Detroit over a century ago, the carefully structured coney starts with a steamed bun that is layered, in order, with a natural-casing hot dog—the kind with a good snap when you bite it, meat-only chili, chopped sweet white onions, and yellow mustard. Variations of the coney dog have their fans in Flint, Jackson, and elsewhere. But it's the Detroit coney that has stood the test of time.

In 1917, Greek immigrant Constantine "Gust" Keros opened his American Coney Island in downtown Detroit where it stands today. Gust's brother William started the city's coney war by opening rival Lafayette Coney Island next door. Legions of coney connoisseurs prefer Duly's Place, a simple, stand-alone diner that opened in 1921 in southwest Detroit. Anthony Bourdain famously declared it his fave and featured it on his show *Parts Unknown*.

American Coney Island
114 W Lafayette, Detroit
313-961-7758
americanconeyisland.com

Duly's Place
5458 W Vernor Hwy., Detroit
313-554-3076
facebook.com/DulysConeyIsland

20

GO TO HELL

FOR A HECK OF A GOOD TIME

A dot on the map named Hell, about a half hour's drive northwest of Ann Arbor, is home to Damnation University, Screams Souvenirs and Creamatory ice cream, and a tiny chapel popular with couples who'd sworn it would be a cold day in Hell before they'd exchange vows. There are a couple explanations for the origin of the town's name, which was founded in 1838, but the current population has fun with it. You can pay to be the Mayor of Hell for a day, buy a square inch of Hell, and send postcards from Hell, complete with singed edges.

Smitty's Hell Saloon serves up good food and drinks, with a sense of humor. Start with the Inferno Dip or Broom (bread) Stix, and move on to the Buzzard Reuben, Italian Witch sandwich, or Hell Hole Nachos. It's also known for its fish, pasties, pizza, and, yep, a helluva Bloody Mary.

You can go from Hell to Paradise in one day. It's a 340-mile drive between Hell and the small UP community on Lake Superior.

Screams Souvenirs from Hell & Helloween
4045 Patterson Lake Rd., Hell, 734-878-2233
gotohellmi.com

Smitty's Hell Saloon
4095 Patterson Lake Rd., Hell, 734-648-0669
facebook.com/HellSaloon

Heavy Metal in Lakenenland, Marquette

MUSIC AND ENTERTAINMENT

21

HAVE A CLOSE ENCOUNTER OF THE BIRD KIND

AT THE DETROIT ZOO

At the world's largest penguin facility, the state-of-the-art, 33,000-square-foot Polk Penguin Conservation Center at the Detroit Zoo, you'll almost feel as if you're stepping into the arctic home of the more than 80 resident chinstrap, gentoo, king, macaroni, and rockhopper penguins. Massive windows give a good overview as they hop, waddle, socialize, and swim in their chilly white surroundings, where the air temperature is 37 degrees Fahrenheit and the water about 40 degrees Fahrenheit. With snow- and ice-making machines, and rocks and ice hand-sculpted of concrete to look like elements of their natural habitat, the environment is designed to encourage penguins' wild behavior. A standout feature is the 326,000-gallon pool that, at 25 feet deep, allows diving and porpoising. On a stroll through two acrylic tunnels surrounded by water, you can observe the underwater activity. To interact directly with the penguins, book a breakfast meetup or a two-hour behind-the-scenes tour.

8450 W 10 Mile Rd., Royal Oak, 248-541-5717
detroitzoo.org

FOLLOW HOLLAND'S YELLOW BRICK ROAD

When author L. Frank Baum and his family lived in Chicago, they summered near Holland in Macatawa, at the Lake Michigan shore, from 1899 to 1910. Anecdotes indicate that elements of his book *The Wonderful Wizard of Oz*, which was published in 1900, were inspired by his observations of Michigan people and places. As a tribute to Baum and the book, the folks of Holland have installed a yellow brick road that connects Oz-themed gardens and art. In Centennial Park, there's a giant living mosaic book made of 6,000 plants. Across the street, bronze sculptures of Dorothy and Toto, Tin Man, Scarecrow, Cowardly Lion, a Munchkin, a Flying Monkey in a tree, and the Wicked Witch grace the grounds of the Herrick District Library. The sculptures are based on the book's original artwork by W. W. Denslow, so the characters look a bit different than those in the 1939 *Wizard of Oz* movie, but it's still fun for photos.

Centennial Park
250 Central Ave., Holland, 616-394-0000
holland.org/oz-sculpture-garden

23

BE A GREAT LAKES
BOATNERD

In the state surrounded by four of the five Great Lakes, freighter watching is a thing. Fans of the big vessels call themselves boatnerds and follow, photograph, and camp out to capture close-up views. The Soo Locks are a must for marveling at the freighters, and at Marquette's Presque Isle Dock it's possible to catch one loading its cargo of ore pellets. In the far eastern UP, boatnerds head to tiny DeTour's waterfront parks.

You may spot a lake boat traveling under the Mackinac Bridge from Alexander Henry Park in Mackinaw City. In the Thumb, along the St. Clair River connecting Lakes Huron and St. Clair, several parks are top viewing spots. From the Detroit Riverwalk and Dossin Great Lakes Museum at Detroit's Belle Isle Park, the City of Windsor, Ontario, Canada, is the backdrop for passing boat traffic.

DeTour Village
detourvillage.org

Detroit RiverWalk
detroitriverfront.org

Dossin Great Lakes Museum
facebook.com/
DossinGreatLakesMuseum

Michigan's Thumbcoast
bluewater.org

Sault Ste. Marie
saultstemarie.com

Soo Locks Visitor Center
www.lre.usace.army.mil/missions/
recreation/soo-locks-visitor-center

Travel Marquette
travelmarquette.com/things-to-do/
arts-culture/ore-docks

HEED THE CALL OF THE WILD

IN GAYLORD

Michigan is nicknamed "The Wolverine State," but you won't see one of the elusive weasel cousins roaming the woods. You'll have to settle for stuffed at Call of the Wild in Gaylord, where a wolverine taxidermy mount occupies one of the museum's more than 60 dioramas. Most depict Michigan wildlife—black bears, elk, skunks, wolves, and whitetail deer—at home surrounded by elements from their natural environments and engaged in normal behavior, against a beautiful hand-painted backdrop. Sounds of the animals add to the realism of these finely detailed habitats, and they're impressive: think two moose, horns locked in battle, or a family of raccoons posted in a tree.

A scavenger hunt for kids, hands-on activities, and interactive, informational panels make it an educational and entertaining stop for all ages. Call of the Wild opened in 1965, but its roots date to 1957 and the Underground Forest, where Carl Johnson first displayed his collection of stuffed animals. Still family owned and operated, this classic roadside attraction has been an Up North tradition for generations. Allow time to browse the quality gift shop.

850 S Wisconsin Ave., Gaylord, 989-732-4336
callofthewildgaylord.com

25

CLIMB ABOARD
THE POLAR EXPRESS

The Polar Express is real and lives in the city of Owosso. The locomotive that inspired author Chris Van Allsburg's children's Christmas classic *The Polar Express* is a workhorse in the collection of the Steam Railroading Institute in Owosso. The 400-ton steam engine was built in 1941 in Lima, Ohio, and is one of the last of its size still in operation. Its sounds and blueprints were used to create the movie's locomotive on film, and each November and December the *Pere Marquette 1225*, a.k.a. North Pole Express, fills its passenger cars with families on a nostalgic, two-hour Country Christmas excursion. The 1225, which is recognized by the National Register of Historic Structures, also offers fall color tours and themed trips throughout the year. The Steam Railroading Institute owns, restores, maintains, and operates its rolling stock and a museum with exhibits, a model railroad layout, and a collection of artifacts and archival materials.

405 S Washington St., Owosso, 989-725-9464
michigansteamtrain.com

ADDITIONAL TRAIN EXCURSIONS

Coopersville & Marne Railway

Vintage locomotives and 1920s passenger cars on a seven-mile, 90-minute trip between Coopersville and Marne in West Michigan.

mitrain.net

Little River Railroad

A 100-year-old steam locomotive departs Coldwater pulling cars from the turn of the last century, 1920s, '30s, and '40s.

littleriverrailroad.com

Southern Michigan Railroad

Fall color and other themed trips between Clinton and Tecumseh.

southernmichiganrailroad.com

26

FEEL THE BEAT
AT THE MOTOWN MUSEUM

In 1959, on an $800 loan from his entrepreneurial parents, Detroit autoworker and songwriter Berry Gordy Jr. launched not just a record company but a musical movement. In an unassuming house nicknamed "Hitsville U.S.A.," Gordy developed the distinctive, danceable Motown sound, described as soul music with pop appeal, and added well-choreographed dance routines and dazzling, coordinated costumes. The revolutionary performances crossed racial lines and launched the careers of Stevie Wonder, Diana Ross and the Supremes, Smokey Robinson, the Temptations, Four Tops, the Jackson 5, and so many others. Open 22 hours a day, the hit factory turned out "Baby Love," "My Girl," "I Heard It Through the Grapevine," and dozens more now-classic tunes. A guided tour of what is now the Motown Museum takes you from the company's humble origins in Gordy's upper flat, where the family's dining table served as the label's shipping department, through exhibits of memorabilia, photos, glitzy costumes, and the original recording equipment in Studio A. A major expansion of the museum is underway, pausing the tour schedule. Check website for special events.

2648 W Grand Blvd., Detroit, 313-875-2264
motownmuseum.org

SEE OUTSIDER ART INSIDE

AT SHRINE OF THE PINES

Tucked into the woods on the Pere Marquette River, just south of the village of Baldwin, the Shrine of the Pines Furniture Museum houses the incredible creations of self-trained artist Raymond "Bud" Overholzer. Bud was a guide for hunters and fishermen for most of the year, but in his three months off he handcrafted rustic furnishings and fixtures out of what remained after the forests had been cleared during the logging industry's heyday. As his tribute to the trees, from the 1930s until his death in 1952, Bud gathered white pine stumps, limbs, and roots, and transformed them into organic works of functional art. His ingenuity starts at the 300-pound front door, which is made of pine logs and turns without effort on a wooden ball. Among the 201 pieces: a huge sideboard carved from a single trunk; a seven-foot-in-diameter table crafted from a 700-pound stump; and a rocking chair that rocks 55 times on one nudge. Bud used only hand tools and handmade pegs instead of nails, he concocted his own glue, and he made sandpaper of crushed glass. Open for tours in the warm weather months.

8962 S M-37, Baldwin, 231-745-7892
facebook.com/shrineofthepinesfurnituremuseum

28

CHEER CHERRIES
IN THE CHERRY CAPITAL

The first cherry trees in Michigan were planted in 1852 on Old Mission Peninsula, in the Little Finger of the state. The trees took well to the soil and climate along the Lake Michigan shoreline, and by the early 1900s, tart cherries had blossomed into an industry that thrives today. While Michigan also grows sweet cherries, it is the leading producer of the Montmorency tart variety, and Traverse City has staked its claim as Cherry Capital of the World. Each July the National Cherry Festival, a nearly century-old tradition that started as a Blessings of the Blossoms Festival, has grown into an eight-day extravaganza attended by a half million visitors. The 150 mostly free activities and events include two parades, multiple concerts, activities for the kids, orchard tours, a midway, cherry-pie-eating contests, farmers markets, and two nights of fireworks.

cherryfestival.org

TIP

See acres of cherry orchards in bloom across miles of the Grand Traverse area each spring. The timing depends on the weather and location, but the show usually begins in mid-May.

Download the Blossom Tour Guide and maps at traversecity.com/things-to-do/tours/cherry-blossom-tours

29

DO A WATER DANCE
IN GRAND HAVEN

Inspired by a musical fountain he saw in Berlin while serving in World War II, Dr. William "Bill" Creason decided to bring the concept to his hometown on the Lake Michigan shore. Designed and constructed with private monies by volunteers in 1962, the Grand Haven Musical Fountain mesmerizes audiences every evening from Memorial Day through Labor Day with free, synchronized water and light shows set to a variety of tunes, from country to Motown, with Taylor Swift, Jimmy Buffett, ABBA, Ladies of the 80s, and movie tunes. With recent enhancements, an elaborate, computerized program can require up to 17,000 commands to choreograph a 25-minute, multicolored, dancing water display, which uses 90,000 gallons of water and may take 50–60 hours to produce. Spectators enjoy the show from the Grand Haven Boardwalk, their boats, or the grassy lawn at the Lynne Sherwood Waterfront Stadium on the opposite bank of the Grand River.

1 N Harbor Dr., Grand Haven, 616-935-3272
ghfountain.org

30

WISH UPON A STAR
AT A DARK SKY PLACE

The night sky is a stage for Mother Nature's incredible star shows and the northern lights, especially in areas minimally affected by light pollution. The international DarkSky organization educates and advocates for protection of the night sky from artificial illumination cast by exterior home and other building lights, neon lights, and streetlamps. It certifies places around the world that consciously work to minimize light pollution and awards them DarkSky status. Michigan is home to 10 designated dark sky places: three International Dark Sky Parks, one International Dark Sky Sanctuary, and six dark sky preserves at Michigan State Parks and Recreation Areas. These areas are ideal for stargazing, astrophotography, catching a meteor shower, identifying constellations, and aurora viewing.

Although without official dark sky designations, Michigan has three national parks that offer spectacular viewing: Sleeping Bear Dunes National Lakeshore on Lake Michigan in the northwest area of the Lower Peninsula, and on Lake Superior within Pictured Rocks National Lakeshore and Isle Royale National Park.

State and International
Dark Sky Places
michigan.gov/dnr/places/state-parks/Dark-sky-events
michigan.org/darksky

Isle Royale National Park
nps.gov/isro

Pictured Rocks
National Lakeshore
nps.gov/piro

Sleeping Bear Dunes
National Lakeshore
nps.gov/slbe

31

ROAM THE HOME
OF RESCUED BLACK BEARS

If having your picture taken with a bear cub is on your bucket list, head to Oswald's Bear Ranch. The all-bear sanctuary, on 240 acres southwest of Tahquamenon Falls, is the largest of its kind in the US, and it usually houses 40 bears in their natural environment. In 1997, Dean "The Bear Man" and Jewel Oswald developed the rescue operation for orphaned cubs, which also became a rehab facility for injured bears. Visitors follow paths and climb raised platforms to view and photograph bears at home roaming their roomy (and fenced) habitats. The daily 4 p.m. feeding is a popular photo op. There's a snack bar that sells apples for you to feed to the bears and a mini museum and gift shop for bear souvenirs. Bring cash; no cards are accepted. The proceeds and fees for admission and photos with the cubs support the family-run ranch and an additional 200 acres that will become a bear sanctuary away from public view. Seasonal.

13814 County Rd. 407, Newberry, 906-293-3147
oswaldsbearranch.com

PULL A TRIP TO THE MAGIC CAPITAL

OUT OF YOUR HAT

Each summer, magicians and fans make their way to the village of Colon, the Magic Capital of the World, for Abbott's Magic Get Together. The four-day event brings together top talent and aspiring magicians who perform at ticketed and free shows, indoors and out. A highlight is the guided tour of Lakeside Cemetery, the final resting place of more than three dozen magicians, including Harry Blackstone Sr. It was the famed 20th-century magician who put Colon on the map when Harry and his wife, Inez, bought property on Sturgeon Lake in 1926. He and his troupe and other performers vacationed in the tiny town, located about halfway between Detroit and Chicago. Among them was Australian Percy Abbott, who came for the fishing, married a local woman, and in 1934 opened the magic shop that still bears his name. Today there are three magic shops in Colon, and the Colon Community Historical Museum has displays about the area's magical connections.

124 St. Joseph St., Colon, 269-432-3235
abbottmagic.com, magicgettogether.com

TIP

The American Museum of Magic in nearby Marshall is built on an extensive private collection of magic memorabilia and artifacts, costumes, photographs, posters, and books. Check the website for magic shows, tours, and lectures.

107 E Michigan Ave., Marshall, 269-781-7570
americanmuseumofmagic.com

33

GET READY FOR YOUR CLOSE-UP

AT A MOVIE LOCATION

Michigan is the location for dozens of movies, scrappy indie productions, and features with big-name stars, including *Hoffa* (Jack Nicholson), *Beverly Hills Cop* (Eddie Murphy), *Out of Sight* (George Clooney, Jennifer Lopez), *Gran Torino* (Clint Eastwood), and Eminem in *8 Mile*. The Pure Michigan website provides downloadable booklets online for several movies with self-guided tours to film locations, including anecdotes about the making of the movies and tips on other sights to see in each area. The featured films include *Anatomy of a Murder* (1959), a courtroom drama starring Jimmy Stewart and Lee Remick, which was inspired by an actual murder trial and shot in and around Marquette. The time-travel romance *Somewhere in Time* (1980), set at Grand Hotel and filmed around Mackinac Island, stars Christopher Reeve and Jane Seymour. In Detroit and the movie-set town of Mason, the sci-fi *Real Steel* (2011) has ex-boxer Hugh Jackman dealing with a young son and boxing robots.

Michigan Film & Digital Media Office
michigan.org/film

TIP

Each October, Grand Hotel fills with guests dressed in 1912 garb for the Somewhere in Time Weekend. Fans of the romantic film hold discussions about the production, view a special screening, visit film locations, and don period clothing for cocktail receptions, dinner, and the Costume Promenade. Grand Hotel makes the movie available for guest viewing throughout the season, and one of its suites is dedicated to *Somewhere in Time*. The movie is shown weekly on the big screen in the theater at Mission Point Resort, where many film scenes were shot.

grandhotel.com

missionpoint.com

SAIL AWAY
ON GRAND TRAVERSE BAY

Sample the romance and relaxation of the inland seas under the billowing sails of the Schooner *Manitou*, a 114-foot replica of a 19th-century vessel typical of those that would have traveled the Great Lakes. The Traverse Tall Ship Company offers a variety of scheduled, two-hour outings on Grand Traverse Bay aboard the 58-passenger schooner. Families favor the afternoon Moomers Ice Cream Sail, while adults may prefer a brunch or evening wine-tasting sail. On the cruise Nibi: The Spirit of Water, guide Tera John of the Grand Traverse Band of Ottawa and Chippewa Indians explores the connection between the Anishinabek and the bay. The local band Song of the Lakes livens up select evening cruises with their jigs and sea shanties. All are welcome to help by hoisting a sail or taking the helm to steer the schooner. Multiday windjammer cruises are also offered, and the sailing yacht *Scout* is available for two-hour and six-hour private charters, for up to six passengers.

13258 SW Bay Shore Dr., Traverse City, 231-941-2000
tallshipsailing.com

MARVEL
AT MOTHER NATURE'S ART

Towering up to 200 feet above Lake Superior, the colorful and sculpted sandstone cliffs of Pictured Rocks National Lakeshore are stained by seeping minerals and shaped by weather and erosion into formations nicknamed Miners Castle, Indian Head, and Battleship Row. The national park stretches 42 miles, from the western gateway at Munising eastward to Grand Marais. Its forested 73,000 acres are home to secluded beaches, waterfalls, inland lakes, and the spectacular Grand Sable Dunes. With nearly 100 miles of hiking trails, there are options for all abilities, from short accessible paths to rigorous wilderness treks, and there are rustic drive-in campgrounds and primitive backcountry sites.

Admire the extent of nature's beauty from the water on a three-hour, narrated outing with Pictured Rocks Cruises, guiding excursions since the 1940s. Riptide Ride offers a zippier alternative on open-air jet boats that circle Grand Island, where colorful rocky wall art soars 300 feet above Munising Bay.

Grand Sable Visitor Center
E21090 County Rd. H-58, Grand Marais, 906-494-2660

Pictured Rocks Cruises
100 City Park Dr., Munising, 906-387-2379
picturedrocks.com

Munising Falls Visitor Center
1505 Sand Point Rd., Munising, 906-387-3700
nps.gov/piro

Riptide Ride
1309 Commercial St., Munising, 906-387-8888
riptideride.com

LET A CAROUSEL
TAKE YOU FOR A RIDE

If going around in circles astride a work of art is your thing, hop on a painted pony and go for a spin on the Silver Beach Carousel in St. Joseph. The nostalgic ride operates year-round in a glass-walled house at the Lake Michigan shore, where Silver Beach Amusement Park was a destination for Chicago tourists and locals from the 1890s until closing in 1971. The original Silver Beach merry-go-round was sold, but locals raised funds to build a replacement, and the current carousel whirled into action in 2010. Its 20 horses, including replicas of some from the original 1910 ride, are accompanied by a menagerie of zoo animals. All were carved from basswood using traditional turn-of-the-century patterns and poses, then assembled with only glue and colorfully painted and bejeweled. Stationary chariots offer riders accessible options. Of the two band organs pumping out "A Hot Time in the Old Town" and "Let Me Call You Sweetheart," one is from the original Silver Beach Carousel.

333 Broad St., Saint Joseph, 269-932-1141
silverbeachcarousel.com

MORE PLACES TO GO ROUND AND ROUND IN THE MITTEN

Dearborn—Greenfield Village

thehenryford.org

Detroit RiverWalk

detroitriverfront.org

Flint—Crossroads Village

crossroadsvillagecarousel.com

Grand Rapids Public Museum

grpm.org

Holland—Nelis' Dutch Village

dutchvillage.com

Holland—Windmill Island Gardens

facebook.com/WindmillIsland

37

ADMIRE THEIR
HEAVY METAL ART

A giant steering wheel with the slogan "Onaway Steers the World" greets visitors to Awakon Park in what was once the home of the American Wood Rim Company, maker of wooden steering wheels and bicycle rims. The tribute to Onaway was crafted by Tom Moran, a self-taught welder who founded his successful Moran Iron Works in his hometown, in the northeastern LP. When he's not fabricating boats or industrial equipment, Tom creates large sculptures, some of which are displayed in the free park, including towering busts of the Statue of Liberty, Abraham Lincoln, and Michigan's own President Gerald Ford.

In the UP, between Munising and Marquette, Lakenenland is populated by metal monsters, aliens, dinosaurs, critters, musicians, and salutes to the military, miners, and lumberjacks. Over the course of a few decades, welder Tom Lakenen has created more than 100 colorful characters out of scrap and repurposed materials; he calls it "Junkyard Art." Some are whimsical; some make political statements. They line the walking/driving trail through the woods of his 37-acre free sculpture park, which is open 24/7 year-round and is on the North Country Trail and a snowmobile route.

Awakon Park
Washington St., Onaway
onawaymi.com/awakon-park

Lakenenland
2800 M-28 E, Marquette
lakenenland.com

HEAR STARS UNDER THE STARS AT INTERLOCHEN

In a wooded, 1,200-acre lakeside setting south of Traverse City, the Interlochen Center for the Arts is a destination for students and lovers of the arts. Founded as a music camp in 1928, the summertime Interlochen Arts Camp now draws more than 3,000 students from around the globe, and the Interlochen Arts Academy is a boarding high school for young people, who come to learn, perform, and develop their talents in music, theater, visual arts, dance, creative writing, and filmmaking. The public is welcome to attend free and ticketed programs by guest artists and Interlochen students and faculty at dance performances, recitals, concerts, plays, film screenings, and readings. The historic Interlochen Bowl dates to 1928 and is the outdoor setting for concerts and performances. Kresge Auditorium is the largest venue, with nearly 4,000 seats under a covered pavilion. It's where the biggest names in the summer arts festival perform, such as Jason Mraz and Interlochen alumni Norah Jones and Jewel.

4000 J. Maddy Pkwy., Interlochen, 231-276-7200
interlochen.org

39

LOCK THROUGH
AT THE SOO

You don't have to be a deckhand on a Great Lakes freighter to travel through the Soo Locks in Sault Ste. Marie. The world's busiest lock system, by cargo tonnage, allows vessels of all sizes to navigate the 21-foot difference in water levels between Lakes Superior and Huron, including the popular boat tours that give civilians an up-close look at the engineering marvel, sometimes alongside the big ships. The first substantial lock was built in 1855, with increasingly larger locks constructed to accommodate ships up to 1,000 feet long. The locks operate with a system of gates, gravity, and valves that control water depths to lift and lower vessels to lake levels.

Displays at the free Soo Locks Visitor Center describe the process, and there's an elevated platform for watching freighters "lock through." The locks close annually from January 15 to March 25. Boat tours operate from mid-May to mid-October.

Famous Soo Locks Boat Tours
515 E Portage Ave., Sault Ste. Marie, 906-632-2512
soolocks.com

Original Soo Locks Boat Tours
1157 E Portage Ave., Sault Ste. Marie, 906-632-6301
originalsoolocktours.com

Soo Locks Visitor Center
312 W Portage Ave., Sault Ste. Marie, 906-253-9290/906-259-2841
www.lre.usace.army.mil/missions/recreation/soo-locks-visitor-center

BAKE!
WITH ZING

You may have heard of Zingerman's, the destination for foodies who have been flocking to Ann Arbor since 1982 when the original Delicatessen opened in a 1,000-square-foot storefront. It's received national recognition as one of "America's Best Jewish Delis" according to *Food & Wine* magazine, and it still serves made-to-order sandwiches and carries select grocery and pantry items in a much-expanded space. The Zingerman's empire has grown, too, and includes the full-service Roadhouse restaurant; Next Door Café; Bakeshop for breads and pastries; Coffee Company roastery and Coffee Bar; the Creamery's fresh cheese and gelato; handcrafted sweets from the Candy Manufactory; and Miss Kim, a Korean restaurant.

You can experience Zingerman's magic in a hands-on baking or cooking class at BAKE! Bakehouse. Master your choice of dozens of recipes, from croissants, bagels, rye bread, and cakes to soups, pasta, and chicken potpie in three- to four-hour sessions. Or, make it a week- or weekend-long BAKE-cation in Ann Arbor.

BAKE!
3723 Plaza Dr., Ann Arbor, 734-761-7255
bakewithzing.com

Zingerman's
zingermans.com

41

EXPERIENCE A GRAND ART ADVENTURE
AT ARTPRIZE

When it launched in Grand Rapids in 2009, ArtPrize was called a "radically open international art competition" that welcomed the art by any artist aged 18 and up, from anywhere on the planet, working in any medium. Submissions range from small ceramics to towering sculptures, huge murals, and interactive experiences. For 16 days each September, the works are displayed at venues throughout the designated ArtPrize district, at just about any business or site that asks to host a work—museums, yes, but also churches, pubs, hotel lobbies, cafés, shops, and parks.

The number of entries has topped 1,100, from 50-plus countries, displayed at some 180 locations around town. Visitors, as well as judges, vote for winners of large cash awards in several categories. It's also a culture event with arts workshops, music, a makers market, parades, and fireworks. ArtPrize put Grand Rapids on the art community's map and draws an estimated 700,000 visitors each year.

artprize.org

ABSORB ACOUSTIC EXCELLENCE AT ORCHESTRA HALL

It took about six months to build a home for the Detroit Symphony in 1919, and nearly 20 years to restore it when Orchestra Hall was saved from destruction in 1970. The acoustically perfect, 2,000-seat beaux arts building was designed by theater architect C. Howard Crane. It served the city's acclaimed orchestra and welcomed guest artists including Enrico Caruso, Richard Strauss, and Pablo Casals until 1939, when the symphony was forced to leave Orchestra Hall. From 1941 to 1951, it was known as the Paradise Theatre, a premier jazz club whose stage was graced by the likes of Duke Ellington, Louis Armstrong, Ella Fitzgerald, Lena Horne, and Pearl Bailey. By 1970, the theater was in ruins, but in its 11th hour local bassoonist Paul Ganson rallied a community of supporters who raised funds and donated countless hours to its restoration. The Detroit Symphony returned to Orchestra Hall in 1989, where it performs today. The DSO calendar features classical, pops, and jazz series, family concerts, and special events.

3711 Woodward Ave., Detroit, 313-576-5111
dso.org

Higgins Lake, Roscommon

SPORTS AND RECREATION

43

CLIP-CLOP INTO THE PAST:
DRIVE YOUR OWN HORSE AND BUGGY

On Mackinac Island, where cars are banned, you can get around by walking, bicycling, or taking a horse-drawn taxi. But at this place where horse is king, you also have the option of hitting the trails on a guided or independent saddle ride. Cindy's Riding Stable and Jack's Livery Stable have horses for hire, and Jack's also offers the chance for you to take the reins of your own horse-drawn carriage around the island—no experience required. Trot back in time on a drive along the 8.2-mile perimeter road that circles the island, or head into the interior park to follow park roads through the woods on a romantic ride for two or a jaunt for four. Jack's Livery Stable is a fourth-generation business with reliable horses that the knowledgeable staff match to your level of expertise. You'll receive brief driving instructions, horse-handling tips, a map, and suggested routes based on your interests and length of the outing.

Jack's Livery Stable
7754 Mahoney Ave., Mackinac Island, 906-847-3391
jacksliverystable.com

Cindy's Riding Stable
7447 Market St., Mackinac Island, 906-847-3572
cindysridingstable.com

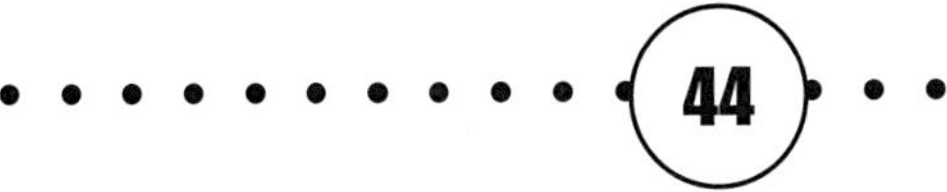

RIVERWALK
IN THE MOTOR CITY

The transformation of Detroit's riverfront over the past two decades has been remarkable. Through a coalition of government, private, and foundation support, what was a hardworking industrial eyesore is now a public gathering space linking parks, plazas, green spaces, sculptures, and gardens. The Detroit RiverWalk is striding toward completion of its eventual 5.5 miles, stretching from the city's Belle Isle Park westward to the Ambassador Bridge, the international link with Windsor, Ontario, Canada.

The site that at one time was the world's largest tire manufacturing plant is now the Uniroyal Promenade. All along the waterway, where there were abandoned warehouses, railroad tracks, parking lots, and factories, bicyclists, pedestrians, and runners now share the wide, paved path; people relax on benches to watch freighters pass by; kids splash in fountains and ride the colorful carousel; families picnic and fishers try their luck at the state park; concert music wafts from the amphitheater; Detroit River boat tours depart; and Great Lakes cruise-ship passengers disembark for tours.

detroitriverfront.org

DIP YOUR PADDLE
IN CRYSTAL-CLEAR WATERS

For thousands of years, Indigenous people navigated the waters of the Great Lakes region in dugout and birchbark canoes. European missionaries, explorers, and fur traders traveled by them. Paddling has progressed from a means of survival to commercial and recreational use, and kayaks and paddleboards have joined canoes as popular forms of human-powered transportation. Michigan is a three- (some say four-) season paddler's paradise, with 11,000 inland lakes and 36,000 miles of navigable rivers and streams in addition to Lakes Erie, Huron, Michigan, and Superior. There are countless ways to get out on the water, whether you prefer the solitude of a silent sports lake, a guided kayak brewery tour in Traverse City, an urban excursion on the international waters of the Detroit River, or a trip alongside freighters through the Soo Locks. Some spectacular sights, like Lake Huron's Turnip Rock off the top of the Thumb, are accessible only by kayak. Michigan Water Trails is mapping more than 3,000 miles of trails with information on navigating the waterways and points of interest en route.

michigan.org/paddle-sports

Michigan Water Trails
michiganwatertrails.org

TIP

Kayak the Canadian Soo Lock and experience the 21-foot drop in water levels between Lakes Superior and Huron, just like the freighters. Some kayaking experience is recommended for the guided tour.

Bird's Eye Outfitters
107 E Portage Ave., Sault Ste. Marie, 906-259-7121
birdseyeoutfitters.com

46

DUNE SCOOT
WITH MAC WOOD

Michigan's more than 300,000 acres of sand dunes, shifting mountains of sand that tower up to 450 feet above the Great Lakes, are generally accessible only by foot. But at Silver Lake Sand Dunes along Lake Michigan on the Mitten's west coast, you can experience the thrill of skimming over the vast, desertlike expanses on Mac Wood's Dune Rides in Mears. The guided tours were the brainchild of resort owner Malcolm "Mac" Wood, who wanted to keep his guests entertained. In 1930, he adapted a Model A that could drive on dry sand and was powerful enough to carry four passengers up and down the natural roller coaster. He called it a Dune Scooter for the way it handled the sand. Still a family operation, Mac Wood's cherry-red, 20-passenger, open-air vehicles make the seven-mile, 40-minute excursions several times a day from mid-May through September. The rides are suitable for all ages; no reservations accepted. Saugatuck Dune Rides offers a similar experience a little farther south, on Michigan's Art Coast.

Mac Wood's Dune Rides
629 N 18th Ave., Mears, 231-873-2817
macwoodsdunerides.com

Saugatuck Dune Rides
6495 Blue Star Hwy., Saugatuck, 269-857-2253
saugatuckduneride.com

DRIVE THE SAND MOUNTAINS AT SILVER LAKE

If you've taken the Mac Wood or Saugatuck sand dune rides and were bitten by the dune scootin' bug, you may want to experience the thrill of driving your own off-road vehicle across the sand mountains. It's allowed at one place in Michigan, the only dunes east of the Mississippi where it's possible: Silver Lake State Park. Of the park's 3,000 acres, 2,000 are sand dunes, and the designated ORV scramble area occupies 450 of those, including a piece of the park's three-mile stretch of Lake Michigan shoreline. The ORV area is not a flat, sandy beach. Expect hills and a challenge in climbing the highest dunes. But that's the fun of off-roading.

In addition to the park's Recreational Passport, your vehicle, whether a motorcycle, ORV, ATV, or UTV, must display an ORV license and trail permit and 10-foot-tall orange safety flag (available at local stores). If you don't have a qualifying set of wheels, you can rent them locally. Find complete rules, regulations, and tips at the website below. Open seasonally.

8960 W Fox Rd., Mears, 231-873-3083
michigan.gov/dnr/things-to-do/orv-riding/silver-lake

FISH
THE HOLY WATER

The famed Au Sable, one of the premier trout fishing rivers in the country, flows 138 miles through the northern LP and the towns of Mio, Roscommon, Grayling, and Oscoda, where it feeds into Lake Huron. The river has three branches: the north, south, and main, known as the "Holy Water." That eight-mile tract is for catch-and-release-only fly-fishing and is a destination for trout anglers who hail from Maine, Montana, and beyond. It's where Trout Unlimited was founded in 1959, by a group of sportsmen concerned about conservation and protection of wild and native trout and their rivers and streams.

Gates Au Sable Lodge is at the heart of it all, perched on the banks of the river near Grayling since 1970. The fly shop stocks everything you'd need and more, staffed by people who know what they're doing. Full-time, fly-fishing professionals offer on-stream instruction for beginners and lead wade trips and float excursions in Au Sable riverboats. Motel rooms are simple, comfortable, and come with a tying table and view of the river, just yards away, tempting you to wade in at dusk to spend an evening angling.

471 Stephan Bridge Rd., Grayling, 989-348-8462
gateslodge.com

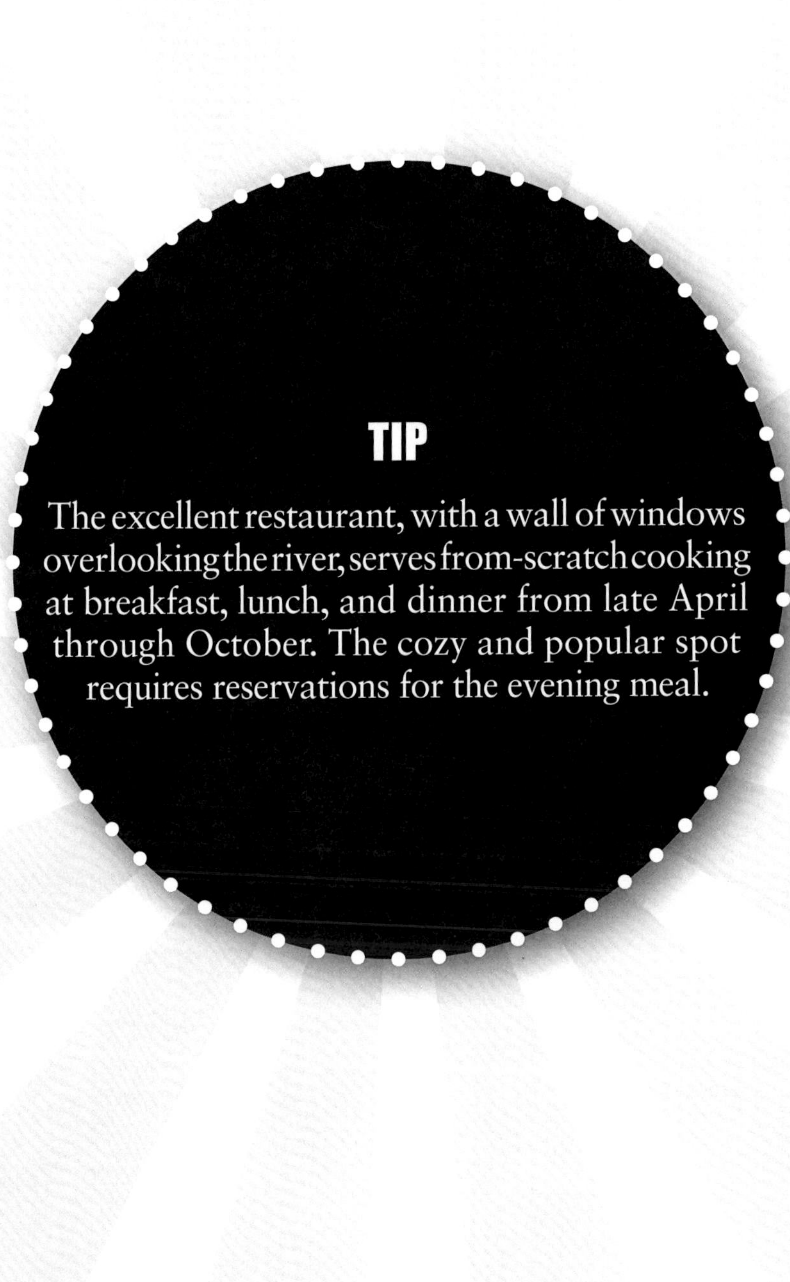

TIP

The excellent restaurant, with a wall of windows overlooking the river, serves from-scratch cooking at breakfast, lunch, and dinner from late April through October. The cozy and popular spot requires reservations for the evening meal.

49

GRAB YOUR BEACH TOWEL
AND HEAD TO THE WEST MICHIGAN PIKE

"Unsalted and Salt Free" is declared on T-shirts with an outline of Michigan and the Great Lakes. With nearly 3,300 miles of shoreline there's no shortage of freshwater beaches to choose from, and each has its special appeal. Do you prefer sand for sunning and castle building? A rocky shore for agate, Petoskey stone, and Yooperlite hunting? Nearby the amenities of a town or remote for the solitude? Sunrise or sunset?

So much shoreline, so little time. One place to start: the seven waterfront communities of the Beachtowns along the West Michigan Pike. The "Pike" is a Lake Michigan–hugging route developed in 1911 in the early days of automobile travel. Stretching from the Indiana border to Mackinaw City, it was designed to convince Chicagoans to spend time (and tourist dollars) in "Michigan's Summerland" enjoying the beaches and breezes. Several of the Pike's Beachtowns consistently rank among the top beach destinations in the US. Start exploring with the downloadable guide and map and prepare for spectacular sunsets.

michiganbeachtowns.com

TIP
The state has 21 designated Pure Michigan Byways, and many boast Great Lakes beaches.
Download the "Pure Michigan Driving Guide" for maps and info at michigan.org/explore-pure-michigan-byways

DIVE
INTO SHIPWRECK ALLEY

Off the Sunrise Side of Michigan's Mitten, more than 100 lost vessels rest in Lake Huron waters up to 210 feet deep, earning the area the name "Shipwreck Alley." They're protected by the Thunder Bay National Marine Sanctuary in Alpena, one of 16 designated National Oceanic and Atmospheric Administration marine sanctuaries. It is also a state Underwater Preserve. Thunder Bay is a popular spot for divers of different skill levels because some of the wrecks are in shallow water and accessible to snorkelers.

The Marine Sanctuary is headquartered at the Great Lakes Maritime Heritage Center, a free gem of a museum that features the exhibit "Exploring the Shipwreck Century." Climb aboard a replica of the wooden schooners that once traveled the Great Lakes and get a taste of the perils of sailing Lake Huron during a storm.

Thunder Bay National Marine Sanctuary
500 W Fletcher St., Alpena, 989-884-6200
thunderbay.noaa.gov

Michigan Underwater Preserves
michiganpreserves.org

TIP

Stay dry and spy sunken vessels on a two-hour Alpena shipwreck glass-bottom boat tour. In season, they depart from the Heritage Center on the Thunder Bay River.

888-469-4696
alpenashipwrecktours.com

When in the UP, see sunken vessels in Lake Superior on the two-hour Glass Bottom Boat Shipwreck Tour of Munising Bay.

1204 Commercial St., Munising, 906-387-4477
shipwrecktours.com

TAKE YOUR SLEDDING
TO THE NEXT LEVEL

Learn to luge like an Olympian. Of the four luge tracks in the US that are open to the public, two are in Michigan: Negaunee's Lucy Hill in the UP and Muskegon Luge on the western edge of the Mitten. Both welcome newbies, provide gear, and instruct you on how to control the sled with your feet, hands, and body before sending you sliding down the track.

Lucy Hill is a *naturbahn* luge, the only competition track for natural luge in the US. Athletes in training reach speeds of up to 50 mph on the snow-packed and icy, half-mile course that follows the natural terrain downhill; the public takes a shorter track reserved for beginners. At Muskegon Luge Adventure Sports Park, the 850-foot track, with its six curves, is a *kunstbahn* (artificial track) made of natural snow and ice. Riders use an authentic luge-training sled handcrafted in Austria. Winter activities at the Muskegon park also include sledding, ice-skating, cross-country skiing, and snowshoeing.

Lucy Hill
230 E County Rd., Negaunee, 906-250-1813
upluge.org

Muskegon Luge
462 N Scenic Dr., Muskegon, 877-879-5843
msports.org

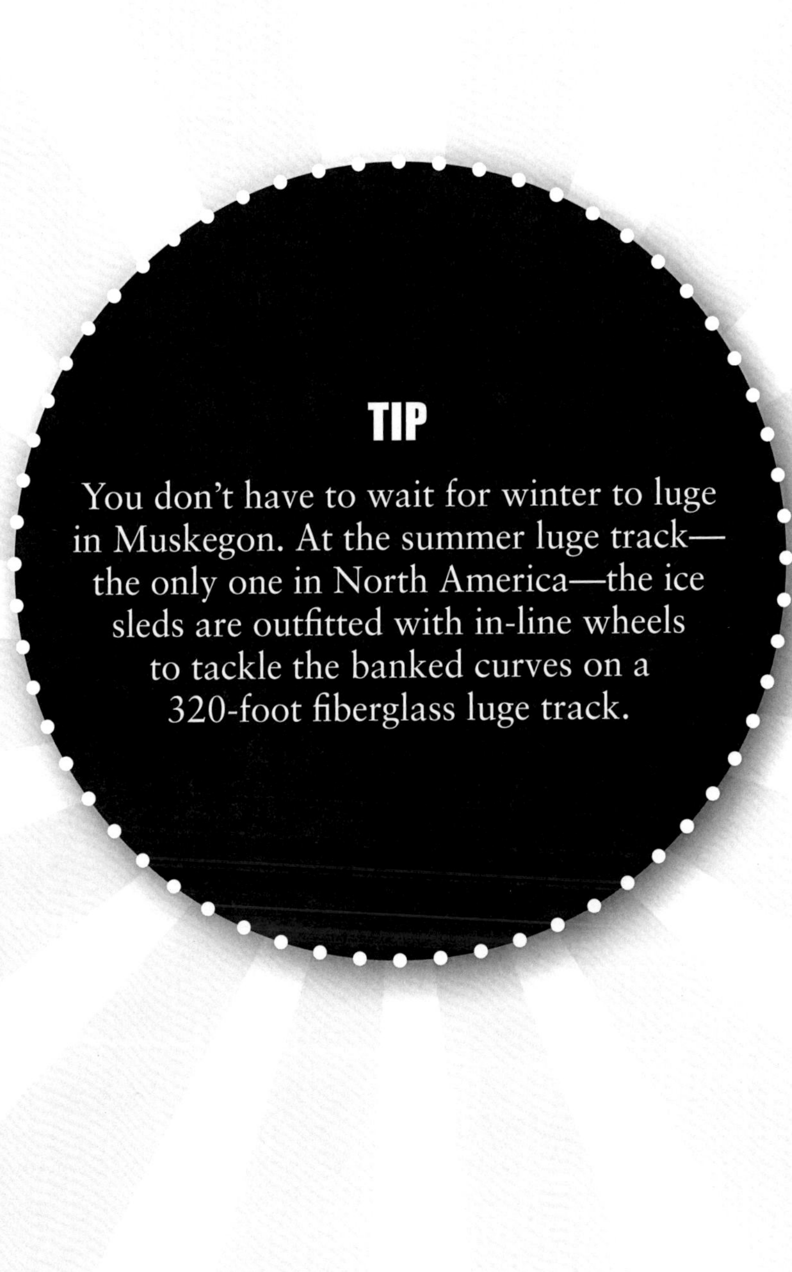

TIP

You don't have to wait for winter to luge in Muskegon. At the summer luge track—the only one in North America—the ice sleds are outfitted with in-line wheels to tackle the banked curves on a 320-foot fiberglass luge track.

52

WAKE UP TO THE BEAUTY
OF SLEEPING BEAR DUNES

The Anishinabek legend of Sleeping Bear tells of a mother bear and two cubs that swam from Wisconsin across Lake Michigan. Within view of land, the exhausted cubs drowned, and the mama collapsed on shore, mourning her lost children. Two islands emerged marking the spots where the cubs disappeared and are now known as North and South Manitou Islands. At Sleeping Bear Dunes National Lakeshore, the massive mountains of sand mark the spot where the grieving mother bear kept watch over them. The Dune Climb is a must-do, but scrambling up the hot, slippery sand is more strenuous than it may appear. At the top, the view is of beautiful Glen Lake. Gravity helps with the trip back down.

Take a hike through the woods and dunes of the Empire Bluff and Pyramid Point Trails for views of Lake Michigan, and splash in its waters at a choice of beaches along 35 miles of shoreline. The 71,000-acre national park also protects cultural attractions including the historic maritime village of Glen Haven, where the Sleeping Bear Inn is again welcoming overnight guests.

Philip A. Hart Visitor Center
National Park Entrance Pass required.
9922 Front St., Empire, 231-326-4700
nps.gov/slbe

Hop into your vehicle for the seven-mile Pierce Stocking Scenic Drive with twelve designated stops, starting with a covered bridge photo op and highlighted by the Lake Michigan Overlook with its sweeping, spectacular view from high above the inland sea.

ENJOY SNOWMOBILING
ALL YEAR LONG

With Michigan's 6,500-plus miles of groomed snowmobile trails and an extensive, interconnected trail system, sledding is big, especially in the UP, which claims about 3,300 of those miles. You don't have to be a sledhead to appreciate the Top of the Lake Snowmobile Museum in Naubinway, 45 minutes west of St. Ignace. Volunteers have built a showcase for antique and vintage snow machines, "Where the history of snowmobiling comes to life." Some of the 200 "old and odd" sleds are on permanent display and others, on loan from about 50 collectors, rotate out. Exhibits explain that the first snow vehicles were built to aid the fishing and forestry industries and evolved from commercial to recreational use. You'll learn that a conversion kit could replace a 1926 Model A Ford's tires with skis and tracks to make it snow ready, and in the 1950s and '60s, countless tinkerers built sleds like the Waywego to roar across the white stuff. The wide array of colorful snowmobiles from the sport's 1960s–70s heyday is eye-popping. Open year-round.

Top of the Lake Snowmobile Museum
W11660 US-2, Naubinway, 906-477-6298
snowmobilemuseum.com

Michigan snowmobile info
michigan.gov/dnr/things-to-do/snowmobiling

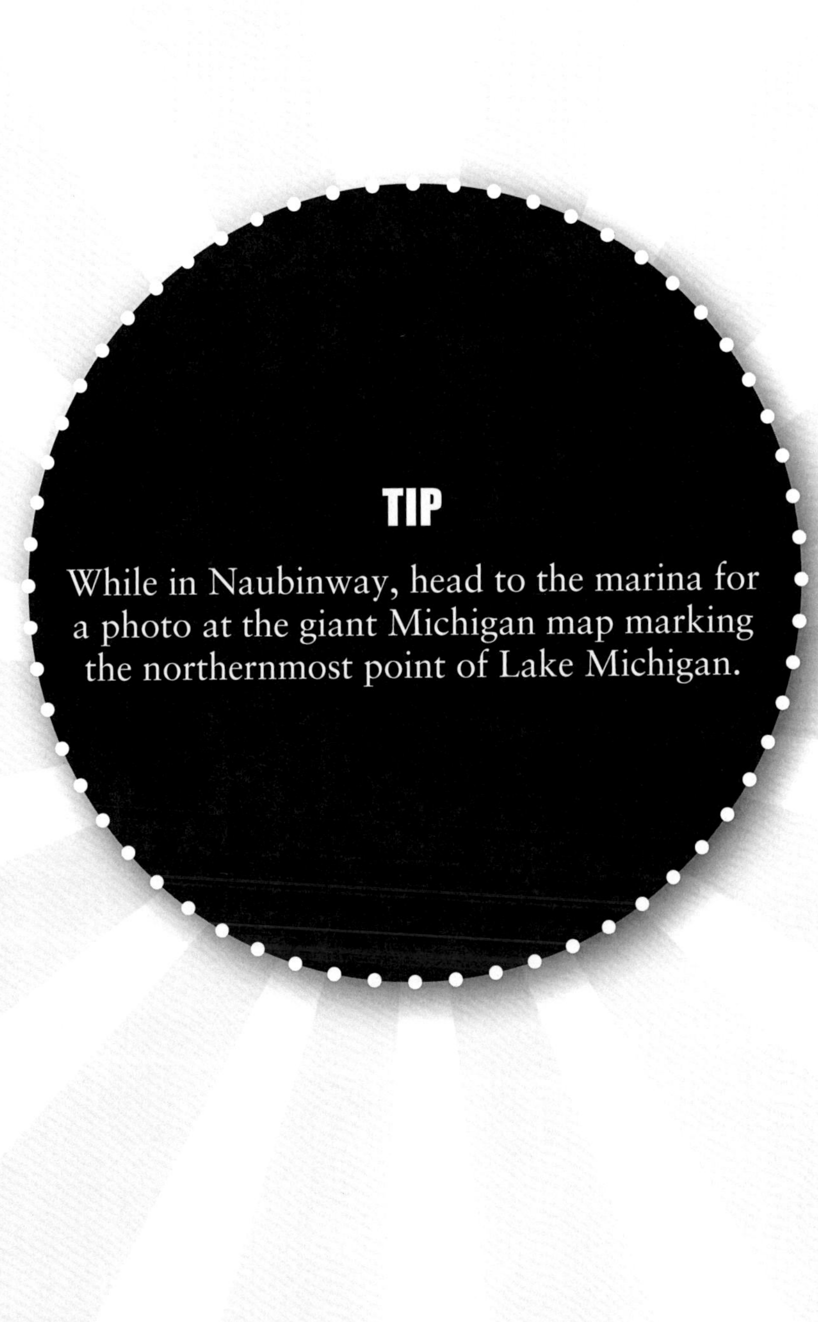

TIP

While in Naubinway, head to the marina for a photo at the giant Michigan map marking the northernmost point of Lake Michigan.

54

TIPTOE THROUGH THE TREETOPS
ON A SKYWALK

If a hike in the woods brings you closer to nature, has health benefits, and is downright enjoyable, why not elevate that experience on a stroll with a bird's-eye view of the flora and fauna from the Mitten's three skywalks? The longest canopy walk in the US is in Midland's Whiting Forest of Dow Gardens. The 1,400-foot-long, multidimensional walkway meanders through red pine and spruce trees at heights from 25 to 40 feet above the forest floor. The Canopy Walk consists of a traditional solid catwalk, a cargo-net rope bridge, viewing platforms, sculptural pods, and a glass-floored overlook. At the 755-acre Hidden Lake Gardens southwest of Ann Arbor, the 374-foot Canopy Walk is a peaceful stroll through the woods at a height of 65 feet. SkyBridge Michigan at Boyne Mountain Resort is the world's longest timber-towered suspension bridge. It's a scenic chairlift ride to the summit and 1,200-foot-long bridge with a section of glass floor for panoramic views of the Boyne Valley 118 feet below.

All are accessible and open year-round (weather dependent).

FIND THE PERFECT VIEW

Boyne Mountain Resort SkyBridge Michigan

1 Boyne Mountain Rd., Boyne Falls, 855-688-7024
boynemountain.com/skybridge-michigan

Dow Gardens Whiting Forest Canopy Walk

1809 Eastman Ave., Midland, 800-362-4874
dowgardens.org/forest

Hidden Lake Gardens Canopy Walk

6214 Monroe Rd. (M-50), Tipton, 517-431-2060
facebook.com/hiddenlakegardens

GO WILD
AT ISLE ROYALE NATIONAL PARK

Rugged and remote Isle Royale in Lake Superior is a spiritual place and an important part of the ancestral land and culture of the Grand Portage Band of Lake Superior Chippewa. Over the centuries, white settlers discovered what the Anishinabek knew, and the 400-island archipelago became a commercial fishing center further developed by lumbering, mining, and tourism. Of the national parks, Isle Royale is one of the system's least visited in the lower 48 states. Fewer than 30,000 adventurers make their way by boat or seaplane to the 45-mile-long island, 55 miles from the Keweenaw Peninsula, during its mid-April through October season. There are 165 Wi-Fi-free miles of wilderness hiking trails, solitude, scenery, and wildlife sightings—the island is the home of the Wolf–Moose Project, a long-running predator–prey study. Paddling is popular, boat tours make scheduled excursions, and water taxis shuttle between points of interest. Backpackers sleep at designated campgrounds and cross-country camping zones, and the Rock Harbor Lodge, with lodging and dining spots, provides rustic comfort.

906-482-0984
nps.gov/isro

Transportation:
Ranger III: nps.gov/isro
Isle Royale Queen IV: isleroyale.com
Isle Royale Seaplanes: isleroyaleseaplanes.com

Landmark Books, Traverse City

Ziibiwing Center, Mt. Pleasant

Kayak Rental, Port Austin

DeVries & Co., Eastern Market, Detroit

Agate Rock Hound, Grand Marais

Wilson's Cheese Shoppe, Pinconning

Pointe Aux Barques Lighthouse

Germack, Detroit

Lake Superior Whitefish Point

Sweetie-licious, DeWitt

Shoreline Pasty Picnic

Mackinac Island Pedal Power

Delaware Mine Ruins, Keweenaw

Gerald R. Ford Presidential
Museum & Library, Grand Rapids

Meats & Mooore, Bay City

Call of the Wild Museum, Gaylord

MAKE A SPLASH
AT AN INLAND LAKE

In the Great Lakes State, it's the freshwater seas Erie, Huron, Michigan, and Superior that get most of the attention. But Michigan also counts 11,000 inland lakes with their own appeal and array of four-season recreational options. In addition to swimming and beaching it, inland lake lovers enjoy all manner of watercraft and fishing for more than 150 species. In the wilderness or resort areas, each lake has its individual beauty and personality. Depending on the lake's size, depth, and weather conditions, water colors can range from turquoise to very dark blue. And there are chains of lakes, notably in the Coldwater area near the Indiana border; the Inland Waterway from Lake Huron at Cheboygan to Crooked Lake; and the Cisco Chain of Lakes sharing the border with Wisconsin.

No boat? No problem. Rentals make it possible to cruise spring-fed, crystal-clear Higgins Lake on a pontoon; troll Lake Gogebic, the UP's largest inland lake; and everything in between. Check with the tourism office in the area you're visiting.

Search "inland lakes" at michigan.gov/dnr
and
Pictured Rocks National Lakeshore at nps.gov/piro
Sleeping Bear Dunes National Lakeshore at nps.gov/slbe

57

FIND YOUR NEW PAPERWEIGHT
AT A GREAT LAKE

With more than 3,000 miles of Great Lakes shoreline, rockhounding is a natural for serious collectors and novices of all ages. With its geological history and the glacial movement that created the lakes, Michigan is rich in its variety of specimens. Topping the rock charts are the Petoskey stone, a fossilized coral found largely along the Mitten's Lake Michigan shoreline, and colorfully banded agates on Lake Superior. The hot rock of the moment is sodalite-rich syenite, which requires a night hike because it looks gray by day but transforms into an otherworldly, fluorescent-orange-glowing rock under a UV light. Discovered in recent years on Lake Superior, they were dubbed Yooperlites by the rockhound who first found them. Other popular finds are Isle Royale greenstone, the state's gemstone; pudding stones; jasper; Leland Blues; and quartz. One of those rocks has been waiting billions of years for you to find it, so grab your bucket and go. Even if you spend the day picking "oh so pretty" stones, you'll enjoy meditative time by the water and go home with a new paperweight.

Michigan Rockhounds
michiganrockhounds.com

TIP

Collecting is not allowed at national parks and historical sites. Collecting is limited to 25 pounds of rock, mineral, or fossil per person each year. Best times for beachcombing are in the spring and after a storm, when the water and sand have been churned up.

See the ones that got away at the A. E. Seaman Mineral Museum, Michigan's official mineral museum, at Michigan Tech University.

1404 E Sharon Ave., Houghton, 906-487-2572

museum.mtu.edu

FALL FOR ELK
IN THE BIG WILD

The Pigeon River Country State Forest, about 115,000 acres located northeast of Gaylord, is home to one of the largest free-roaming elk herds east of the Mississippi. Called "The Pigeon" or "The Big Wild," it's your best bet for viewing the magnificent animals in, well, the wild. Late September through early October at dawn and dusk is prime elk-peeping time, when bulls are in the mating mood, rounding up cows and feeding in open fields. Listen for their bugle call, which could be a message to a potential mate, or a warning to another bull. Once native to the state, elk disappeared in the 1800s, but a century of conservation efforts has brought the herd to an estimated 900–1,200 animals. Bring the binoculars and keep your distance. Bulls can weigh between 375 and 1,000 pounds and should not be approached.

Don't count on GPS or cell service. Fill the gas tank and download and pack a paper map; print Michigan's Elk Viewing Guide at michigan.gov/dnr/things-to-do/wildlife-viewing/elk and the Elk Tour Map at pigeonriverdiscoverycenter.org.

Pigeon River Country Discovery Center
9984 Twin Lakes Rd., Vanderbilt
pigeonriverdiscoverycenter.org

TIP

No need to go wild. See elk in the city at Gaylord's Elk View Park, where a herd of about 40 bulls and cows roam the enclosed 108 acres. Parking is next to, what else, the Elks Lodge.

116 Grandview Blvd., Gaylord
gaylordmichigan.net/get-outdoors/elk-viewing-in-the-gaylord-area

GET AWAY
TO THE GEM OF THE HURON

The one-mile car ferry ride from DeTour Village takes a matter of minutes, but the destination might as well be another planet. Drummond Island, at the eastern end of the UP, is a place of rare beauty, with geological features unique to its mostly undeveloped 87,000 acres; nearly 70 percent of the land is state owned. The resident population of fewer than 1,000 is padded year-round with visitors who come to hunt, fish, camp, dive on shipwrecks, stargaze, and bird- and wildlife-watch. The second-largest island in the Great Lakes has a 150-mile Lake Huron shoreline, 34 inland lakes, meadows, forests, cedar swamps, and trails for hiking, snowmobiling, cross-country skiing, and off-roading.

Natural wonders include the 1,210-acre Maxton Plains Preserve, protector of the alvar, one of the world's best examples of ancient limestone habitable only to select plants. It's a rugged drive to Fossil Ledges, the layered remnants of a saltwater coral bed, and to the rocky Steps at Marblehead—a challenge that Jeep drivers welcome. Hunt for a souvenir pudding stone or pick up the conglomerate rock at a local shop. Drummond may be remote, but it has good accommodations, dining options, stores, and historical sites to explore.

Drummond Island Visitor Center
34974 S Townline Rd., Drummond Island, 906-493-5245
visitdrummondisland.com

TIP

See Drummond from the inland sea under the billowing sails of Schooner *Huron Jewel*, a 78-foot-tall ship designed and built by Capt. Hugh Covert and his wife, Julie. Outings range from two- and four-hour sails to overnight trips, including multiday excursions.

906-430-5854
ditallship.com

60

GUSH OVER
AN EPIC WATERFALL OR 200

Henry Wadsworth Longfellow's 1855 epic poem *The Song of Hiawatha* tells the tale of an Ojibwa named Hiawatha and his love for Minnehaha. The setting is the south shore of Gitche Gumee—Lake Superior—and Taquamenaw, the Tahquamenon River and Falls. The Upper Falls, at 200 feet wide with root-beer-colored water rushing over its 50-foot drop, is the largest of Michigan's more than 200 named waterfalls. Tahquamenon's brown hue comes from tannic acid seeping from surrounding cedar, hemlock, and spruce trees, and depending on the season, it flows at up to 50,000 gallons per second. It's an impressive sight and just a short walk on a paved path to viewing areas as well as two platforms, each at the bottom of about 100 steps. Four miles downstream in the 46,000-acre Tahquamenon Falls State Park, the gentler Lower Falls is a series of five small cascades that are approachable by renting a rowboat or crossing the accessible pedestrian bridge to a small island.

Both Upper and Lower Falls entrances are
off M-123 northeast of Newberry.
906-492-3415
Search "Tahquamenon Falls State Park"
at michigandnr.com/parksandtrails

TIP

The beauty and bounty of waterfalls flow westward from Pictured Rocks National Lakeshore to Porcupine Mountains State Park on Lake Superior. Many are accessible by paved paths or short trails; others require a hike. Ocqueoc Falls in the northeastern LP is the only named waterfall below the Mackinac Bridge. It's universally accessible with a paved path and ramp into the river for kid-friendly swimming.

Check with the tourism offices in the areas you're visiting; some have waterfall maps.
Search "UP waterfalls" at uptravel.com
Search "Ocqueoc Falls" at us23heritageroute.org

Greenfield Village, Dearborn

CULTURE AND HISTORY

61

CROSS THE MIGHTY MAC,
A POEM IN STEEL

More than a means of transport, the Mackinac Bridge is a symbol of the state and engineering marvel that designer Dr. David B. Steinman aptly called "a poem in steel." Both graceful and powerful, the twin-towered suspension bridge opened in November of 1957 and is the physical link between the state's two peninsulas. "Mighty Mac" carries an average of 11,000 vehicles a day over its five miles spanning the Straits of Mackinac, where the waters of the Great Lakes Huron and Michigan mingle. Before the bridge was built, ferries shuttled travelers between Mackinaw City in the LP and St. Ignace in the UP, causing miles-long traffic backups during peak periods.

The toll is based on type of vehicle. Rather not drive the span? A Bridge Authority employee will take the wheel of your vehicle for a small fee. The bridge is closed to vehicles one day a year, as tens of thousands of pedestrians participate in the annual Labor Day Mackinac Bridge Walk. At other times, hikers, snowmobilers, and bicyclists pay a fee to hitch a ride with the bridge transport service.

906-643-7600
mackinacbridge.org

MIGHTY MAC STATS

Length of bridge: 26,372 feet

Height of twin towers above water: 552 feet

Roadway width: 54 feet

Height of roadway above water at midspan: 199 feet

Depth of water below bridge: up to 295 feet

Length of wire in main cables: 42,000 miles

Diameter of main cables: 24.5 inches

Weight of bridge: 1,024,500 tons

Number of rivets: 4,851,700

Number of bolts: 1,016,600

Number of workers who built it: 3,500 at site; 7,500 at mills, quarries, and shops

Average number of daily crossings: 11,000

62

APPRECIATE THE ANISHINABEK,

MICHIGAN'S FIRST PEOPLE

The stories of Michigan's first people are told at several locations across the state including two significant cultural institutions, the Ziibiwing Center of Anishinabe Culture and Lifeways in Mt. Pleasant, in the middle of the Mitten, and the Museum of Ojibwa Culture in the UP city of St. Ignace. Founded by the Saginaw Chippewa Indian Tribe of Michigan, the Ziibiwing Center's permanent exhibit *Diba Jimooyung* (Telling Our Story) does so through dioramas, artifacts, and interactive displays in 15 areas that explore the history of the Anishinabek people, their teachings, means of survival, the environment, arrival of Europeans, and identity. The center also hosts changing exhibits and special events.

The Museum of Ojibwa Culture features exhibits in a former mission chapel and grounds with a sculpture park, the Clan Park, which describes the clan system, each represented by an animal, and a longhouse where events are held. It is adjacent to Mission Park and the grave site of Father Jacques Marquette.

Museum of Ojibwa Culture
500 N State St., St. Ignace
906-643-9161
museumofojibwaculture.net

Ziibiwing Center of Anishinabe
Culture and Lifeways
6650 E Broadway Rd., Mt.
Pleasant, 989-775-4750
sagchip.org/ziibiwing

TIP

The Mackinac Island Native American Cultural History Trail consists of six descriptive markers along the perimeter road, and the Native American Museum at the 1830 Biddle House interprets the life of the Anishinabek of northern Michigan.

mackinacparks.com

Sanilac Petroglyphs Historic State Park, in the Thumb, is the state's largest-known collection of Native American petroglyphs, which were carved into the stone 600–1,000 years ago.

michigan.gov/mhc/museums/Sanilac

63

TOUR THE SPLENDOR
OF MICHIGAN'S CAPITOL

Lansing's landmark, the graceful dome of Michigan's capitol building, was a groundbreaking design in 1871 when architect Elijah E. Myers modeled the Renaissance Revival structure after the United States Capitol as an homage to the post–Civil War nation. The 267-foot-high cast-iron dome is the crowning glory of the government seat. Dedicated on January 1, 1879, it is recognized as a National Historic Landmark for its dazzling array of Victorian decorative arts.

Myers fools the eye with painted pine woodwork that looks like pricey walnut and cast-iron Corinthian columns with faux marble finish. Color runs rampant throughout the nine-plus acres of hand-painted art.

View the elegant, 160-foot-high rotunda at the heart of the building from balconies that circle the soaring space, or, as school kids on class trips do, by lying on the lit-from-below glass-block floor and looking up into the spectacular "eye" of the dome.

Free, hour-long guided tours are offered Monday through Friday, and the first Saturday of each month. Or pick up a brochure and building map and explore on your own.

100 N Capitol Ave., Lansing, 517-373-2353
capitol.michigan.gov

GO BOODLIN'
ON BEAVER ISLAND

It's a two-hour-plus passenger/car ferry ride from Charlevoix near the Tip of the Mitt to Lake Michigan's largest island, Beaver Island, known as the Emerald Isle for the Irish fishermen who settled there in the 1840s. With a year-round population of about 600, there's just one village, St. James, named after self-appointed Mormon King James Jesse Strang. He and a small band of followers arrived in 1848, intent on establishing a utopian community. In 1856, the monarch was murdered and the experiment came to a dark end. The Old Mormon Print Shop Museum tells stories of the island's Mormon, Native American, and Irish heritage.

Laid-back and quirky, activities are low-key. Go boodlin', the locals' term for roaming the island with no particular plan, or follow the historical society's driving-tour map to lighthouses and other sites. Shop for local art, raise a glass at an Irish pub, hike, paddle, golf, or head to the beach. Watch the sunset, stargaze, and relax. You're on island time.

Beaver Island Chamber of Commerce
231-448-2505
beaverisland.org

DITCH THE PASSPORT:
GO DUTCH IN HOLLAND

The 19th-century windmill is the oldest-working Dutch windmill in the US, the colorfully costumed klompen dancers' clogs are hand-carved of wood, millions of tulips bloom around town each spring, and *Sinterklaas* (Saint Nicholas) joins the holiday festivities.

Holland, in the Mitten's southwest, was settled in 1847 by a band of 54 Dutch Calvinist separatists, and that heritage is found in its architecture, cultural attractions, restaurants, and annual events. The De Zwaan Windmill was the last windmill allowed to leave the Netherlands when it was shipped to Holland in 1964. It still turns and grinds grain into flour, and visitors are welcome to visit it and the flower fields, exhibits, and replica buildings of Windmill Island Gardens. Veldheer Tulip Gardens is a massive tulip farm that sells its bulbs. It's also home to DeKlomp Wooden Shoe & Delft Factory, where you may watch a wood carver turn a block of poplar into the iconic footwear, and artisans create Delftware, the blue-and-white hand-painted pottery. For family fun, head to the amusements, café, and shops at Nelis' Dutch Village.

78 E 8th St., Holland, 616-394-0000
holland.org

TIP

Have a bloomin' good time at the Tulip Time Festival, a nine-day event each May that started in 1929 with the blossoming of 100,000 tulips. The city is filled with millions of the colorful flowers, and activities include parades, Dutch dancers, concerts, a carnival, and much more.

holland.org

66

WALK THROUGH HISTORY
AT THE HENRY FORD

It's just about impossible to capture in one place the breadth of imagination, determination, resourcefulness, and genius that have built America, but automobile pioneer Henry Ford nailed it. In 1929, with Thomas Edison at his side, he dedicated the institution now known as The Henry Ford. Three main components draw more than 1.77 million visitors each year to its 250 acres in Dearborn, a Detroit suburb.

The Henry Ford Museum of American Innovation: a space large enough to showcase everything from clocks, 7,000 Hallmark ornaments, and a 1976 Apple 1 computer to presidential limos and the civil rights icon known as the Rosa Parks bus.

Greenfield Village: 83 significant historic structures were relocated to represent eras and influences in American history, including the Wright Brothers' bicycle shop, Edison's Menlo Park Laboratory, working farms, brick slave quarters, and the home where Noah Webster wrote the first American English dictionary. (See also Eagle Tavern entry.)

The Ford Rouge Factory Tour: starts with a shuttle bus to the Ford truck factory for a multisensory experience and view of the F-150 assembly from an elevated walkway.

20900 Oakwood Blvd., Dearborn, 313-982-6001
thehenryford.org

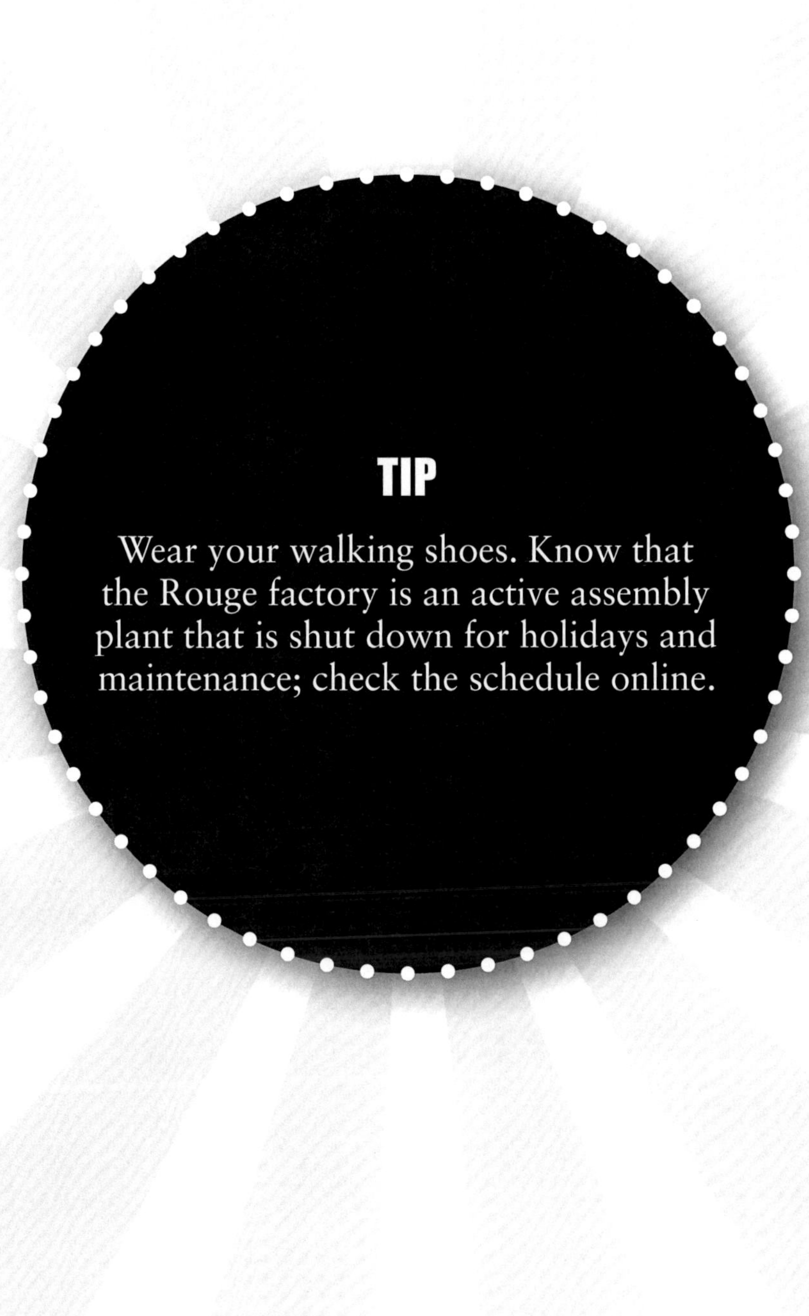

TIP

Wear your walking shoes. Know that the Rouge factory is an active assembly plant that is shut down for holidays and maintenance; check the schedule online.

MEET GERALD R. FORD,
THE NEVER-ELECTED PRESIDENT

Michigan claims one commander in chief: Gerald R. Ford. The official museum of the 38th president of the US is in Grand Rapids, where he grew up and began his political career as a congressman. Through photos, models, displays, clothing, and artifacts, the museum tells his story from his youth through his decision to run for Congress; his elevation in 1973 to vice president under Richard Nixon and then, in 1974, to the Office of the President; his unsuccessful presidential election bid in 1976; and his post-presidential years.

Delve into key moments in the personal and public lives of President Ford and First Lady Betty Ford. Special exhibits include a Watergate gallery and a look at the US bicentennial celebration of 1976. Large-scale highlights are the interactive Cabinet Room and full-scale replica of the Oval Office. The museum and Gerald R. Ford and Betty B. Ford Burial Site are on parklike grounds overlooking the Grand River and downtown Grand Rapids.

303 Pearl St. NW, Grand Rapids, 616-254-0400
fordlibrarymuseum.gov

TIP

The Gerald R. Ford Presidential Library is located 130 miles east of Grand Rapids in Ann Arbor, where he earned a bachelor's degree in economics and played football at the University of Michigan. While his papers and documents are accessible only to researchers by appointment, the exhibits, lectures, and other programs are open to the public.

1000 Beal Ave., Ann Arbor, 734-205-0555
fordlibrarymuseum.gov

68

THINK ABOUT
VISITING THE DIA

The Thinker ponders the stuff of life outside the grand entrance to the Italian Renaissance–style Detroit Institute of Arts. Auguste Rodin's 1903 bronze cast no. 3 moved to Detroit in 1922 and greets visitors to one of the top art collections in the US. Founded in 1855, the DIA's permanent home opened in 1927 and has been expanded three times to accommodate the more than 65,000 works in 140-plus galleries. It is noted for its Modern and Contemporary, Native American, Dutch, Asian, and African American collections.

In 1922, the DIA became the first US museum to acquire a work by Vincent van Gogh, his *Self-Portrait*, painted in Paris in 1887 (with ear intact). The massive *Detroit Industry Murals* by Diego Rivera (1932–33) occupies four walls and was wildly controversial when unveiled. Plan time to view the complex frescoes depicting automobile workers and management interwoven with multiple themes of technology, manufacturing, life, nature, and the environment. Check the DIA calendar for guided tours, Drawing in the Galleries (supplies provided), drop-in workshops, and Friday Night Live! performances.

5200 Woodward Ave., Detroit, 313-833-7900
dia.org

The DIA is the centerpiece of Detroit's Cultural Center, a walkable district that includes the Detroit Historical Museum, Detroit Public Library, Michigan Science Center, and Charles H. Wright Museum of African American History.

visitdetroit.com

69

STEP INTO THE PAST
AT THE MACKINAC STRAITS

The 17th-century Straits of Mackinac saw the arrival of French explorers, missionaries, and the *Griffin*, its first large sailing vessel, plus establishment of the fur trade and French Fort de Buade in St. Ignace. Across the straits, in 1715, the French constructed Fort Michilimackinac, and decades of turmoil and tension between the French, British, and Native Americans followed. By 1781, the British had constructed a strategically safer stone fort on a Mackinac Island bluff overlooking the waterway. It changed British and American hands before being returned to the US after the War of 1812.

Both forts are Mackinac State Historic Parks with costumed interpreters depicting life and times of their eras, and fort buildings feature period furnishings or themed exhibits. At Michilimackinac, it's possible to watch the ongoing archaeological excavation. The effort began in 1959 and has recovered more than a million pieces of the past as well as structural remains that have allowed accurate reconstruction of the 18th-century fort. (Open May–October)

Colonial Michilimackinac
102 W Straits Ave., Mackinaw City, 231-436-4100
mackinacparks.com

Fort Mackinac
7127 Huron Rd., Mackinac Island, 906-847-3328
mackinacparks.com

70

SEE THE SENTINELS
OF THE INLAND SEAS

Some people collect rocks; others collect visits to lighthouses. The Great Lakes State is a destination for lovers of the lights. With 3,200 miles of freshwater shoreline, Michigan has 129 lighthouses, more than any other state. Many of the lighthouses are open to the public, have museum exhibits, and allow a climb to the top of the tower. At several, you may encounter ghost stories of a former lighthouse keeper.

For a deeper dive into the legends and lore of lighthouse living, stay at a beacon-turned-bed-and-breakfast or volunteer to be a lightkeeper. You'll not need to trim lamp wicks or check the lights every four hours as keepers once did, but you may be tasked with tending the gift shop, leading tours, and sweeping the floors. At several, you'll pay for the privilege, but the sights and sounds of the freshwater seas and the possibility of a front-row seat to fierce storms across the water, gorgeous sunrises and sunsets, and dazzling star shows are priceless perks of the job.

Great Lakes Lighthouse Keepers Association
gllka.org

michigan.org/lighthouses

71

HUNT HEMINGWAY'S HAUNTS
IN PETOSKEY

Ernest Hemingway is famously associated with Paris, Havana, Key West, and Pamplona, but Northern Michigan belongs on the list of the author's haunts. Before there was "Papa," there was Petoskey. In 1899, Dr. Clarence and Grace Hemingway built a cottage on Walloon Lake as a summertime escape from their Chicago-area home. It's where young Ernie roamed the woods and learned to hunt, fish, and love the outdoors. He returned to Petoskey in 1919, seeking refuge after being wounded in Italy in World War I. In 1921, he married his first wife, Hadley Richardson, in the nearby village of Horton Bay. It's where he set *The Nick Adams Stories* and *The Torrents of Spring*.

The seasonal Pere Marquette train depot houses the Little Traverse History Museum and the "Hemingway's Michigan Story" exhibit, and plaques on buildings throughout Petoskey's Gaslight District mark the author's hangouts.

Self-guided Hemingway tour brochure:
walloonlakemi.com/ernest-hemingway-in-michigan

Little Traverse History Museum
100 Depot Ct., Petoskey, 231-347-2620
petoskeymuseum.org

Petoskey visitor info: petoskeyarea.com

TIP

At City Park Grill, grab Hemingway's spot at the bar, below the photo of the author. He frequented the saloon when it was known as the Annex, and he mentions it in his short story "Gentleman of the World."

See a statue of Ernie as a young man in the park next to the restaurant, and another of him in later years in Walloon Lake village.

432 E Lake St., Petoskey, 231-347-0101
cityparkgrill.com

72

EXPLORE LOGGING LORE
AT CASTLES AND CAMPS

Michigan's logging industry was lucrative, if relatively short-lived. Forests heavy with 200-year-old white pine trees that stood 200 feet tall and measured five feet in diameter were cleared in the industry's peak period, from 1870 to 1900, when the state led the nation in lumber production.

In Muskegon, the wealth of the era is evident in the Victorian splendor of the neighboring Queen Anne homes of lumber baron Charles H. Hackley and his business partner Thomas Hume. The Hackley house is rich with stained glass and intricately hand-carved wood and depicts the year 1890. The Hume home interprets the post-lumbering era, as the family would have lived in 1920.

At Hartwick Pines State Park and Logging Museum near Grayling, learn how lumberjacks lived and worked; see exhibits, tools, equipment, and a steam-powered sawmill; and spend a quiet moment in the log-made Chapel in the Woods. Follow the accessible trail through some of the park's 49 acres of towering old-growth white pines, the state's official tree.

Hackley & Hume Historic Site
484 W Webster Ave., Muskegon, 231-722-7578
lakeshoremuseum.org

Hartwick Pines State Park and Logging Museum
3612 State Park Dr., Grayling, 989-348-2537
michigan.gov/mhc/museums/hp

LOG ON

Estivant Pines Nature Sanctuary

Hiking or snowshoe trails through old-growth forests with pines more than 125 feet tall.

On Burma Rd. near Copper Harbor, 866-223-2231
facebook.com/MNAEstivantPines

Porcupine Mountains Wilderness State Park

35,000 acres of old-growth forest with sugar maple, eastern hemlock, and yellow birch.

33303 Headquarters Rd., Ontonagon, 906-885-5275
www.dnr.state.mi.us/parksandtrails/Details.aspx?id=426&type=SPRK

Tahquamenon Logging Museum

Artifacts of the lumber era and monthly summertime lumberjack breakfasts from a wood stove in the cook shack.

7964 M-123, Newberry, 906-293-3700
loggingmuseum.com

CRUISE
INTO MICHIGAN'S MARITIME HISTORY

Surrounded by four inland seas, Michigan's industrial growth and cultural story are rooted in its relationship to the Great Lakes and its centuries-long maritime history. In addition to the Great Lakes Maritime Heritage Center, museums across the state chronicle this freshwater legacy. At the Michigan Maritime Museum in South Haven, have a tall ship adventure on *Friends Good Will*, a replica of a topsail sloop that played a role in the War of 1812. It's one of five watercraft that make scheduled and charter excursions on the Black River and Lake Michigan. Exhibits include a 1939 fish tug and four wooden Coast Guard rescue boats.

The Great Lakes Shipwreck Museum sits at Whitefish Point, at the eastern end of an 80-mile stretch of Lake Superior known as the Shipwreck Coast. Centerpiece of the exhibits and artifacts is the bell recovered from the ore carrier SS *Edmund Fitzgerald*, which sank 17 miles off Whitefish Point on November 10, 1975, with all 29 hands lost.

Michigan Maritime Museum
260 Dyckman Ave., South Haven, 269-637-8078
michiganmaritimemuseum.org

Great Lakes Shipwreck Museum
18335 N Whitefish Point Rd., Paradise, 888-492-3747
shipwreckmuseum.com

FOR MORE ABOUT THE INLAND SEAS

Dossin Great Lakes Museum

Take the wheel of the pilot house of the freighter SS *William Clay Ford* overlooking the Detroit River.

100 Strand Dr., Belle Isle, Detroit, 313-833-1805
detroithistorical.org/dossin-great-lakes-museum

Icebreaker Mackinaw Maritime Museum

Tour the US Coast Guard vessel that served 62 years breaking ice on the lakes.

707 N Huron Ave., #2, Mackinaw City, 231-436-9825
themackinaw.org

Museum Ship Valley Camp

Roam the crew's quarters and maritime artifacts in the cargo hold of the hardworking 550-foot freighter-turned museum.

501 E Water St., Sault Ste. Marie, 906-632-3658
saulthistoricsites.com

Port of Ludington Maritime Museum

Interactive activities and exhibits fill three levels of a former US Coast Guard station on the Lake Michigan shore, in the home port of the SS *Badger* car ferry.

217 S Lakeshore Dr., Ludington, 231-843-4808
ludingtonmaritimemuseum.org

SS *Milwaukee Clipper*

A Great Lakes passenger/auto liner with staterooms, a dance hall, a movie theater, and dining spots is undergoing renovation to its 1940s glory.

2098 Lakeshore Dr., Muskegon, 231-299-0784
milwaukeeclipper.com

MINE THE HISTORY
OF COPPER COUNTRY

Michigan's copper boom in the UP's Keweenaw Peninsula was an important and lucrative industry from the start of large-scale mining in 1845 through the late 1800s, when "Copper Country" supplied the US with 75 percent of its red metal. Immigrants poured in to do the hard labor, while copper cash built beautiful homes for mining executives and the ornate buildings of the bustling City of Calumet.

The copper era ended in 1968, but its legacy is preserved by the Keweenaw National Historical Park, which connects 22 independent Keweenaw Heritage Sites. The visitor center in Calumet has three floors of exhibits that explore the industry and the cultural and human aspects that came with the mix of ethnicities with their own languages, churches, saloons, social activities, and traditions. Take a ranger-led walking tour of downtown Calumet for an introduction to your self-guided tour of sites that include mines, mining communities, and museums. Find suggested driving-tour itineraries at nps.gov/kewe/planyourvisit/trip-itineraries.htm.

98 5th St., Calumet, 906-483-3176
nps.gov/kewe

TIP

If time is short, take in the three floors of exhibits at the park's Calumet Visitor Center and tour one of the mines, each offering a different experience: Adventure Mining Company (adventureminetours.com); Delaware Copper Mine (delawareminetours.com); Painesdale Mine and Shaft (painesdalemineshaft.com); and Quincy Mine Tours (quincymine.com).

75

TRY BACK-IN-TIME ISLAND TIME
ON MACKINAC ISLAND

To the Anishinabek-Ojibwa people, the speck of an island in the Great Lakes waterway between the LP and the UP was an important gathering and sacred place, and home of the Great Spirit Gitche Manitou. They named the land rising from the waters where Lakes Huron and Michigan meet *Michilimackinac*, Land of the Great Turtle. Mackinac Island's story involves centuries of voyageurs, missionaries, fur traders, and the military. By the 1880s, attention turned to welcoming Victorian visitors in search of clean air, natural beauty, and fudge.

Step back in time on a day or (preferably) overnight trip to a place where cars are banned and getting around is on foot, bicycle, or horse-drawn carriage. History lives on in streets lined with pastel-colored shops, lodgings, and cottages, and at Fort Mackinac, high on a limestone bluff, but more than 80 percent of the 2,200-acre island is an undeveloped state park. Make time to explore the diverse ecosystem of meadows, forests, and geological formations including the famed Arch Rock.

Passenger ferries to the island depart from Mackinaw City and St. Ignace. For more about visiting this special place, see Kath's book *100 Things to Do on Mackinac Island Before You Die*.

Mackinac Island Tourism Bureau
mackinacisland.org

76

LOOK TO THE SKY
AT THE AIR ZOO

Climb into an airplane cockpit, thrill to a full-motion flight simulator; lift off on the indoor hot-air balloon ride; admire artist Rick Herter's 32-by-800 foot *Century of Flight* mural, declared by Guinness in 2004 as the world's largest indoor hand-painted mural. The Air Zoo is an aerospace experience for all ages. Opened to the public in 1979 as the Kalamazoo Aviation History Museum, it began with one couple's interest in World War II aircraft. In 1959, Marine Air Corps veteran Pete Parish and Suzanne Parish, who served with the Women Airforce Service Pilots (WASPs), got their collection off the ground with a half investment in an airplane. They eventually launched their museum with a small "zoo" of aircraft with animal names, including a Wildcat, Hellcat, Bearcat, and Flying Tiger.

Several expansions later, the Air Zoo is affiliated with the Smithsonian and occupies two sites, with the main exhibits and amusements at the Flight Innovation Center and well-regarded restoration center at the nearby Flight Discovery Center.

6151 Portage Rd., Portage, 866-524-7966
airzoo.org

HAVE
AN ERIE ADVENTURE

Lake Erie's water laps against a relatively short stretch of coastline in the southeast corner of the state, from the Ohio border to the mouth of the Detroit River. Not as splashy as Michigan's other Great Lakes, it has its low-key charms. Find sandy beaches, world-class walleye fishing, bird-watching, easy walking trails, and other year-round activities at William C. Sterling State Park and Lake Erie Metropark, where the Marshlands Museum explores the flora, fauna, and history of the area.

Nearby Monroe is the site of River Raisin National Battlefield Park, which was the scene of an important and bloody War of 1812 battle—and American defeat—in January of 1813. It gave rise to "Remember the Raisin," the first such rallying cry of the US military. Catch the informative film, exhibits, and interpretive programs at the visitor center, and follow the accessible Battlefield Loop Trail with historical markers.

exploremonroemi.com

TIP

Monroe is the major city in the area and was the home of General George Armstrong Custer. In downtown Monroe, a statue of Custer on his horse depicts him during the Civil War as he led the Michigan Cavalry Brigade into the Battle of Gettysburg.

SURROUND YOURSELF
WITH CREATIVITY AT CRANBROOK

Tucked away in a northern suburb of Detroit, Cranbrook Educational Community is a center for art, science, and instruction that began as a dream of philanthropists and newspaper family George Booth and Ellen Scripps Booth. In 1904, they purchased farmland where they launched a place for creative pursuits and instruction. Named for the Booth family's roots in Cranbrook, England, it has evolved into a 319-acre campus with private independent schools and Cranbrook Academy of Art, as well as cultural resources that welcome visitors. These include a natural history museum, planetarium, and observatory; a contemporary art museum; historic homes; and dozens of sculptures across gardens and landscaped grounds, notably the striking *Orpheus Fountain* with eight bronze figures by Carl Milles.

Tour three house museums: the Booths' 1908 arts and crafts–style Cranbrook House and surrounding formal and Japanese gardens; Saarinen House, a 1930 art deco jewel among many Cranbrook buildings by Finnish architect Eliel Saarinen; and Frank Lloyd Wright's 1950 Smith House, commissioned by two Detroit public school teachers.

39221 Woodward Ave., Bloomfield Hills, 877-462-7262
cranbrook.edu

STROLL ART IN BLOOM
AT MEIJER GARDENS

A 24-foot bronze horse, carnivorous plants, and a wild meadow are a few of the treasures at the Frederik Meijer Gardens & Sculpture Park, where art, nature, and horticulture are woven into a cultural experience and indoor/outdoor, year-round wonderland for all ages. Opened in 1995 in Grand Rapids, the 158-acre Meijer Gardens was made possible by Fred and Lena Meijer, of the Michigan-based Meijer superstore fame.

The five-story Lena Meijer Tropical Conservatory is home to exotic plants and tropical birds from around the world. Within its 15,000 square feet, you'll also find an arid garden, a Victorian Garden Parlor, a display greenhouse, works by Dale Chihuly, and sculpture galleries.

The Meijer collection of 200-plus sculptures includes more than 50 major works by Claes Oldenburg, Keith Haring, Auguste Rodin, Louise Bourgeois, Nina Akamu, Henry Moore, and more that dot the gently rolling landscape of the sculpture park. Themed gardens include the children's garden with multisensory activities and the Japanese garden, a tranquil spot with waterfalls, a Zen garden, bonsai, sculptures, and an authentic teahouse from Japan.

1000 E Beltline Ave. NE, Grand Rapids, 888-957-1580
meijergardens.org

ADMIRE
DETROIT'S ARCHITECTURAL GEMS

Detroit enjoyed a flurry of construction in the early 1900s that reflected the city's pre-Depression-era wealth. In recent years, century-old buildings have been reborn in grand style, like the Michigan Central train station. Completed in 1913 but abandoned in 1988, it's been renovated by Ford Motor Company as an innovation center in Detroit's historic Corktown.

Step into 1924 and the opening of the elegant 31-story Book Cadillac Hotel, which at the time was the tallest hotel in the world. The completely remodeled Westin property could be credited with leading the way for the transformation of several beautiful commercial buildings into boutique hotels.

In 1928, the magnificent Fisher Building claimed the title of Detroit's largest art object for its incredible vaulted ceiling, intricate mosaics, and hand-painted details. Also that year, the over-the-top Fox Theatre opened as the "most magnificent Temple of Amusement in the World." The art deco Guardian Building, completed in 1929, is notable for its abundance of colorful patterns with Native American and Aztec influences.

For guided architectural tours, search visitdetroit.com

81

PUT IT IN GEAR:
DISCOVER MICHIGAN'S CAR CULTURE

Detroit is known as the Motor City, and there's no shortage of car culture attractions in the metro area, including The Henry Ford museum and Rouge factory tour; Diego Rivera's *Detroit Industry Murals* at the Detroit Institute of Arts; the Ford Piquette Avenue Plant Museum, the birthplace of the Model T; and the Ford House, the Cotswold cottage–style estate of Henry Ford's son Edsel and his wife Eleanor Ford, completed in 1928 in Grosse Pointe Shores.

But the fascination with vehicles isn't limited to the Detroit area. The largest automobile museum in the country, the Gilmore Car Museum, is located in southwestern Michigan. It displays more than 400 vehicles plus permanent and changing exhibits and offers vintage car rides, car shows, and other events. Historic barns, an authentic 1941 diner, a re-creation of a 1930s Shell gas station, and re-created car dealership buildings sprawl across 90 acres in Hickory Corners, near Kalamazoo. (Some exhibits are seasonal.)

Ford Piquette Avenue Plant
461 Piquette St., Detroit
313-872-8759
fordpiquetteplant.org

Gilmore Car Museum
6865 Hickory Rd., Hickory Corners, 269-671-5089
gilmorecarmuseum.org

Edsel & Eleanor Ford House
1100 Lake Shore Rd., Grosse Pointe Shores, 313-884-4222
fordhouse.org

The MotorCities National Heritage Area covers hundreds of auto- and labor-related sites across southeast and central Michigan, ranging from museums and historic homes to industrial plants and cemeteries. Its website is a resource for planning a self-guided road trip.

motorcities.org

82

FIND FINLAND IN THE UP

The UP's forests, farms, and waters look much like Finland, which was comforting to thousands of Finns who emigrated in the late 19th and early 20th centuries to work in Keweenaw Peninsula copper mines. That heritage lives on in the large population with Finnish roots, and at Finnish shops, restaurants, museums, and historical sites. January's Heikinpäivä festival celebrates winter indoors and out, and each June, a bonfire marks Midsummer at the Lake Superior shore.

Houghton and Hancock, linked by the Portage waterway's iconic lift bridge, form the gateway to "Copper Country." In Hancock, street signs bear Finnish names, the Finnish American Heritage Center is a cultural hub, and no one has to ask how to pronounce sauna (SOW-na), the Finnish heat-and-steam bath.

Visit Keweenaw
visitkeweenaw.com/search/?q=Finnish

Travel Marquette
travelmarquette.com

TIP

It's not all about the UP. The LP town of Kaleva, near Manistee and Lake Michigan, takes its name from the Finnish epic poem *Kalevala*, which is depicted in murals in the quirky Bottle House Museum. Finnish American John Makinen constructed his family home in 1941 of 60,000 clear and colored bottles from his pop bottle factory.

kalevamichigan.com

SUOMI (FINLAND) SAMPLER

Keweenaw Peninsula

Finnish American Heritage Center

Historical archive, folk school, book and import store, art gallery, events.

fahc.finlandiafoundation.org

Hanka Homestead Finnish Museum

Authentic hand-hewn home and outbuildings on 1890s subsistence farm.

hankahomesteadmuseum.org

Kuusi Modern Mercantile

Home goods featuring Finnish imports.

kuusimercantile.com

North Wind Books

Finnish imports, candies, and books for all ages.

facebook.com/northwindbooks

Suomi Restaurant

Custardy baked pancake, *pannukakku*, is a favorite.

facebook.com/profile.php?id=100063642426867

Takka Saunas

Traditional Finnish heat-and-steam baths.

takkasaunas.com

Marquette

Nestledown Bed & Breakfast

Nordic decor and hospitality, Finnish breakfasts, and sauna.

nestledownmarquette.com

Touch of Finland

Extensive selection of imported textiles, jewelry, home décor, edibles.

touchoffinland.com

Trenary Toast Cafe

Twice baked *korppu* for dunking in coffee.

facebook.com/trenarytoastcafemqt

Bronner's, Frankenmuth

SHOPPING AND FASHION

83

BUY HANDCRAFTED HISTORY

AT THE HENRY FORD

There are museum gift shops, then there's The Henry Ford. Stores in both the indoor museum and outdoor Greenfield Village carry the expected T-shirts, caps, and branded water bottles, but at these shops you'll find a wonderful selection of books, toys, foods, and decor items related to the exhibits and experiences that cover a couple centuries of American history.

Extra special: Watch artisans at work using historic techniques and materials and take home their Liberty Craftworks creations. The inventory varies but includes handblown glass ornaments and the latest in the series of glass candy canes, linoleum-block note cards printed on historic presses, stoneware mugs with a salt-created rustic glaze (test one out at the Eagle Tavern), and functional and decorative pieces from hand-rolled and hand-painted redware clay. You can even buy skeins of yarn from the Merino sheep raised and shorn at the Firestone (yes, the tire people) farm that was relocated from Ohio.

20900 Oakwood Blvd., Dearborn, 313-982-6001
thehenryford.org

Liberty Craftworks Store in the village and Genius at Play in the museum require admission. You need not pay admission to shop at the general Henry Ford Museum or Greenfield Village stores. But really, you don't want to miss either of these institutions.

HAVE TRIPLE THE FUN

AT THREE ART FAIRS IN ONE

It started in 1960 with an arts and crafts market held during the Ann Arbor merchants' Summer Bargain Days. Despite the snub of the art museum director who said, "No good artist will sit in the street," 132 of them displayed their work and launched an institution in the art fair world. The largest juried art fair in the country, the Ann Arbor Art Fair is actually three independent, concurrent events that morph into one sprawling display of artistic ability. Over three days each July, about a half million people stroll 30 city blocks filled with nearly 1,000 artist booths for the Ann Arbor Street Art Fair, the Original; Ann Arbor State Street District Art Fair (launched in 1967); and the Guild's Ann Arbor Summer Art Fair (established in 1970). Food vendors; live musical performances; hands-on art-creation stations; and activities like sidewalk chalk art, plein air painting, and artisan demonstrations complement the work of top artists from across the US.

Downtown Ann Arbor
theannarborartfair.com

The free, annual *Michigan Art Guide* has a calendar of art fairs and information on galleries, museums, and art centers across the state. Pick up a copy at art sources and tourism info offices or download it at michiganartguide.com.

85

WRITE HOME ABOUT GWEN FROSTIC,

WHERE NATURE IS IN THE CARDS

Count Gwen Frostic (1906–2001) as one of Michigan's natural wonders. She overcame a childhood illness and defied doctors who said she'd never walk, talk, or write again. Gwen went on to pursue her talent in art, interest in nature, and business acumen at a sanctuary she built in 1964 in Benzonia, near the Mitten's Little Finger. Without an architect, Gwen and her contractor created an organic structure of stone, wood, and glass that seemingly sprang from the earth. It was where the artist/writer/naturalist/businesswoman lived, worked, and welcomed visitors from around the globe to her world of fields, woods, water, and creatures that are the subjects of her illustrations and poetry.

Elements of the natural world fill the rambling retail shop overlooking the 15 vintage Heidelberg presses that print the note cards, calendars, books, and other Presscraft Papers goods from Gwen's 2,200 original hand-cut linoleum blocks. The building is on the National Register of Historic Places. Open seasonally.

5140 River Rd, Benzonia, 231-882-5505
gwenfrostic.com

86

WARM UP TO
STORMY KROMER

George “Stormy” Kromer, a semipro baseball player who wore his ball cap to work as a railroad engineer in Kaukauna, Wisconsin, asked his wife to help him with a problem. He’d often lose his hat in the breeze as he leaned out of the train window, so Ida added a band that not only kept the cap on his head but also warmed his ears. The hat was a hit and in 1903, a workwear company was born. Stormy Kromer was based in Milwaukee until 2001, when Jacquart Fabric Products bought and moved the company to Ironwood, in the western UP. There, the iconic wool hats are quality crafted in a range of styles and colors far beyond the iconic red-and-black plaid original. Not just for workers and outdoorsmen anymore, the expanded Stormy Kromer clothing line makes a fashion statement with its coats, jackets, vests, shirts, and accessories for men, women, and children—even pets. Pose for a selfie with the giant Stormy Kromer cap outside of the plant, and take a free tour of the factory, offered once daily, Monday through Thursday. Shop at the factory store Monday through Saturday for current and discontinued items and factory seconds.

1238 Wall St., Ironwood, 888-455-2253
stormykromer.com

87

TRY SOME RETAIL THERAPY
AT THE MERCATO

About a mile from downtown Traverse City, a collection of 19th-century buildings on the sprawling campus of a former state hospital have been revived as the Village at Grand Traverse Commons. When the Northern Michigan Asylum opened in 1885, it embodied the "Kirkbride Plan," a philosophy of healing treatment in an environment of beautiful architecture featuring light-and-airy spaces in a parklike setting. Those design elements survive in the Victorian Italianate–style Building 50, an impressive 380,000 square feet of buff-colored brick topped with distinctive red spires. Head to the eateries and shops of its Mercato for local art, antiques, jewelry, clothing, and home goods at a dozen-plus boutiques tucked into the alcoves and under the brick arches. Don't miss Landmark Books, which specializes in classic literature, poetry, modern fiction, Michigan-centric, and the hard-to-find and out-of-print. Bookseller and author Paul Stebleton is also a collector and seller of vintage typewriters and can supply you with ribbons for your writing machine.

800 Cottageview Dr., Ste. 45, Traverse City, 231-922-7225
landmarkbookstc.com

Roam the Village, stop for a bite or a beverage, and take home local flavors like Left Foot Charley's wine, bags of beans from Higher Grounds Coffee, Earthen Ales beer in cans, and cookies and bread from Pleasanton Brick Oven Bakery.

thevillagetc.com

88

TAKE HOME A TASTE OF DETROIT
FROM EASTERN MARKET

Since 1891, Eastern Market has been an important place for Detroiters to buy produce from local farmers. Each Saturday year-round, the colorful market bustles with activity and the huge, historic sheds are filled in prime months with about 225 sellers and 40,000 shoppers. Beyond fresh vegetables, fruits, meats, and baked goods, vendors sell their honey, maple syrup, preserves, salsas, dressings, and other packaged foods. Seasonally, the Tuesday food market is a smaller version of Saturday's main event, and Sundays are for local artists, jewelry makers, crafters, and musicians.

At 43 acres, it is the nation's largest historic public market district, with more than 150 businesses surrounding the open-air market. It's a hub for the wholesale food industry, as well as for specialty food retailers of spices, nuts, candy, coffee, tea, cheeses, and wine. Galleries, boutiques, and vintage shops, plus eateries, a distillery, and a brewpub, make Eastern Market a destination for shopping, food, and entertainment throughout the week.

Russell St. between Mack Ave. and Gratiot Ave., Detroit

Welcome Center (Saturday, Sunday, Tuesday)
1445 Adelaide (between Sheds 2 and 3), Detroit, 313-833-9300

easternmarket.org

TIP
Find farmers markets throughout the state with the Michigan Farm Fun Directory, available at Michigan Welcome Centers, tourism offices, or to download at michiganfarmfun.com

89

CATCH THE HOLIDAY SPIRIT
EVERY DAY AT BRONNER'S

It's Christmas all year long on a 27-acre chunk of Frankenmuth, the Thumb-area town known as "Little Bavaria." Bronner's CHRISTmas Wonderland is a monumental salute to the holiday, from the grounds decked with an oversized Nativity scene, angels, and a towering Santa Claus to the dizzying array of decorations within the self-described "World's Largest CHRISTmas Store." More than 2 million visitors shop Bronner's 361 days a year (it is closed only on Christmas, Easter, Thanksgiving, and New Year's Day).

Founder Wally Bronner started it all in 1945, painting signs, creating window displays for local merchants, and designing and supplying Christmas decor for town lampposts. In 1954, he opened a holiday store named the way that Wally always spelled the word Christ. The CHRISTmas store is still a family operation and carries more than 50,000 items in its 1.7 football fields worth of retail space (and there's more than double that for behind-the-scenes operations). While Christmas decorations and gifts fill most of the shelves, you'll find plenty to make the other holidays, occasions, and seasons bright.

25 Christmas Ln., Frankenmuth, 989-652-9931
bronners.com

SATISFY YOUR SWEET TOOTH WITH MACKINAC ISLAND FUDGE

If Michigan had an official candy, it would be fudge. The confection connection began in 1887 on Mackinac Island, where the tourism trade was taking off. Sara Murdick's special recipes inspired her husband and son to open a shop to tempt visitors with sweet souvenirs. Murdick's Fudge and a half dozen other candy makers sell so many thousands of pounds of the treat each day that visitors are called fudgies. Just try to resist the mouthwatering aromas as you watch fudge makers stir secret combinations of sugar, cream, butter, and flavorings in copper kettles. At just the right temperature, they pour the fudge onto marble-topped tables to cool, while expertly shaping and paddling it into flat loaves to be sliced into half-pound slabs. Go ahead, have a free sample (or a dozen), bring some home for gifts, and earn your fudgie stripes.

Mackinac Island fudge shops (some have multiple locations):

Joann's Fudge, joannsfudge.com

Kilwins, facebook.com/KilwinsMackinacIsland

May's Candy Shop, mayscandyshop.com

Murdick's Fudge, originalmurdicksfudge.com

Murray Hotel Fudge Company, mymurrayhotel.com

Ryba's Fudge Shops, ryba.com

Sanders on Mackinac, facebook.com/sandersonmackinac

FIND HERITAGE GIFTS
AT THE POLISH ART CENTER

In the early 1900s, Polish immigrants flocked to work in Detroit's auto factories, especially the Dodge Main assembly plant that opened in 1911 in Hamtramck. The Polish population of that enclave boomed and was served by several ethnic churches, newspapers, markets, bakeries, butcher shops, restaurants, bars, funeral homes, and social clubs. Eventually, the Polish populace migrated to the suburbs, and other nationalities moved in.

The once-vibrant Polish community has dwindled to a handful of churches, food shops, restaurants, and the Polish Art Center. Founded in 1958, the import store has been owned and operated since 1973 by Raymond and Joan Bittner and family. When daughter Kathleen Bittner-Koch and her husband Thomas moved Up North to start their Polish Heritage Farm, she opened a satellite of her family's store in tiny Cedar, in the Little Finger. You don't have to be Polish to appreciate the imported foods, linens, folk art, amber jewelry, paper goods, apparel, and beautiful hand-painted Boleslawiec Stoneware found at both locations.

9539 Joseph Campau, Hamtramck, 313-874-2242
polartcenter.com

8994 S Kasson St., Cedar, 231-835-2242
facebook.com/polishart.center.cedar, facebook.com/polishheritagefarm

PUT A CHERRY ON TOP WITH A STOP

AT CHERRY REPUBLIC

In 1989, Bob Sutherland founded the Cherry Republic in his hometown of Glen Arbor, near Sleeping Bear Dunes National Lakeshore, by selling "Life, Liberty, Beaches and Pie" T-shirts from the trunk of his car. He eventually traded his showroom on four wheels for a shop featuring foods made with fruit from local orchards. Today, 200-plus cherry products fill six Cherry Republic stores across the Mitten. They're anchored by the rustic Great Hall of the Republic in Glen Arbor, which is surrounded by perennial gardens, a restaurant, and winery. At the winery, kids can sample cherry soda pop while adults sip wine and hard cider. The Cherry Public House serves lunch, dinner, cherry beer, cherry pie, and cherry ice cream. Take home a growler of beer or cider and a whole pie with your cherry haul from the Hall.

6026 S Lake St., Glen Arbor, 231-226-3014
cherryrepublic.com

Additional Cherry Republic Locations
154 E Front St., Traverse City, 231-932-9205
223 S Main St., Ann Arbor, 734-585-5231
221 Bridge St., Charlevoix, 231-226-3006
925 S Main St., Frankenmuth, 231-226-3039
29 W 8th St., Holland, 231-226-3013

GO NUTS
FOR GERMACK'S

Pistachios were largely unknown in the US in 1912 when Armenian brothers John and Frank Germack arrived in New York at the ages of 12 and 7. They eventually built a business importing olive oils, spices, and foods that appealed to the swell of Turkish, Greek, and Eastern European immigrants to the US. By 1924, the brothers expanded their operation to Detroit, where Frank focused the business on importing and roasting pistachios and other nuts that were new to many in this country. He dreamed up the idea of dying pistachios red, and "Red Lip" pistachio nuts became the hallmark of the Germack company. The product line has expanded to include pumpkin and sunflower seeds, dried fruits, mixes, chocolate-covered nuts, and roasted coffees. The fourth generation of Germacks is overseeing the company, which includes a café and retail store in Eastern Market, just blocks from where the success story began in 1924.

2509 Russell St., Detroit, 313-784-9484
germack.com

POUR ON
THE LIQUID GOLD

Maple syrup is the state's first agricultural crop of the year, with the harvest beginning in February in the LP and running into April in the UP. Michigan syrup makers produce about 90,000 gallons annually, in a lengthy process that requires boiling down 40 gallons of sap to create a gallon of the sweetener. Demand for the "liquid gold" exceeds the supply. There are pancakes and waffles to top and beans to bake, but maple syrup is also an ingredient in candies, cocktails, mustard, and innovative products from companies like Harwood Gold, a maple syrup maker in Charlevoix.

Since 1898, the Parsons family has tapped the trees at Harwood Lake, south of town, and made traditional maple syrup. The fifth generation has added 45 gourmet items like black fig maple spread, award-winning sriracha, and ghost-pepper-infused syrup. Buy "made with maple" goods at the Harwood Gold Store & Cafe, an 1885 building with a pressed-tin ceiling and rustic charm, where you can sip espresso or tea with a sweet treat or savory meat hand pie.

230 Bridge St., Charlevoix, 231-437-3900
harwoodgold.com

95

GET YOUR HANDS ON
MICHIGAN MITTENS

It seems like a natural for a state shaped like a mitten, but it wasn't until 2007 that the idea for wearable, warm, winter Michigan Mittens was hatched. On the road home from their UP cabin, Connie Hahne came up with the concept of printing a map of the LP on one mitten and the UP on the other. Her husband Erich shared her enthusiasm and coined the slogan, "Always Have a MAP on Hand!" After some trial and error in launching their enterprise, the couple tapped the talents of Lisa Angelilli and Peter Boyer, experienced artists, marketers, and co-owners of a southeast Michigan screen-print shop. The joint venture heated up, and Michigan Mittens represented the Great Lakes State at the White House for the 2018 Made in America product showcase. The mittens come in six colors, and the expanded line of Michigan gifts includes oven mitts and tiny cotton scratch mitts for babies.

Check the Michigan Mittens website for retail outlets across the state that carry the line of products.

michiganmittens.com

96

FOLLOW THE TREASURE MAP
AT THE KING OF USED BOOKSTORES

A mural of a work glove, about three stories high, clutches the corner of a worn industrial building just west of downtown Detroit. Signage that once identified the 1905 structure as Advance Glove Manufacturing now reads John K. King Used and Rare Books. John King launched his bookselling business as a teen in 1965 and moved a couple times before settling into the current 30,000 square feet. A million or so volumes fill four floors of the former factory, but there's no database to guide you to the book you're looking for. Just a paper map and sections simply labeled with categories of publications that are shelved in each area. Hand-lettered directional signs help, but if you're stymied in your search, pick up the phone to talk to a staffer with encyclopedic knowledge of the inventory. Or just prowl the aisles for another book, magazine, postcard, or some other prize in print. Don't bother looking for caffeine to fuel your visit; there is no café.

901 W Lafayette Blvd., Detroit, 313-961-0622
johnkingbooksdetroit.com

EXPECT THE UNEXPECTED
AT LEON & LULU

There are lifestyle stores, and there's this treasure trove in Clawson, north of Detroit, occupying a 1941 roller rink with its original wooden floor, disco ball, and vintage skates strung along the walls. Since 2006, the 15,000-square-foot community landmark has been the home of Leon & Lulu, imagined by Mary Liz Curtain and her husband, Stephen Scannell, as "An Adventure in Shopping."

Wander through the dizzying array of home goods, chic women's fashions and accessories, toys, and found objects to the Michigan Store, dedicated to wearables, books, and stuff boosting Detroit and the Great Lakes State. Here, Ann Arbor's renowned Motawi art tile shares space with the work of emerging local artists discovered by Mary Liz.

Humor, color, and surprises saturate every inch of Leon (named for their cat) & Lulu (their dog). Circus banners hang from the trusses, a red 1965 Saab is floor décor. The atmosphere is fun, the goods carefully curated and high quality. "We want to excite and delight our customers, to get a giggle," says Mary Liz. And, perhaps, to leave with a souvenir of the experience. You will. Just roll with it.

96 W 14 Mile Rd., Clawson, 248-288-3600
leonandlulu.com

THREE CATS AT LEON & LULU

But wait! There's more next door in the Clawson Theater building, complete with its faithfully recreated 1941 marquee. Now it's a spot for a taste of Michigan in the inventive meals and adult beverages, and for catching live music, magic shows, circus performances—even country line dancing. "Our goal is to be a good time place," says Mary Liz.

threecatscafe.com

SHOP LOCAL
IN THE GASLIGHT DISTRICT

A resort town since the 1890s, Petoskey has grown into a small city but retains its Victorian-era charm in its downtown Gaslight District, lined with iconic lampposts and turn-of-the-century brick and pastel-hued buildings. Historically, this was a shopping destination for summertime resorters, and today there are more than 170 businesses, services, and one-of-a-kind shops and restaurants. Many are family owned and operated, including American Spoon Foods, maker since 1982 of locally sourced, minimally processed preserves, butters, salsas, and other edibles. Pop into Cutler's for top-name kitchenware and home decor items, and Grandpa Shorter's for Michigan-centric gifts. Take the kids to the Rocking Horse Toy Co. for old-fashioned fun. Allow time to browse two floors of McLean & Eakin Booksellers and soak up the cozy ambiance. At Symon's General Store, pick up gourmet food and wine to enjoy as you catch a free concert at Pennsylvania Park, or a million-dollar sunset over Little Traverse Bay.

Downtown Petoskey
petoskeydowntown.com

Visit Petoskey
petoskeyarea.com

99

BECOME A HISTORY KEEPER
AT ANTIQUES TREASURE TROVES

Spend a summer Sunday browsing the wares of hundreds of antiques dealers at the Allegan Antiques Market at the Allegan County Fairgrounds, south of Grand Rapids. In five large buildings and across the spacious grounds, a mind-boggling array of vintage finds fills booths with glass, pottery, china, kitchenware, jewelry, accessories, clothing, furniture, books, art, sporting goods, signage, and architectural salvage. And more. First held in 1979, it stakes the claim as Michigan's largest antiques show, and its location in the southwest corner of the Mitten makes it a convenient drive for shoppers from Illinois, Indiana, and Ohio. Up to 400 Midwestern dealers arrive with their quality goods on the last Sunday of each month from May through September, rain or shine.

Prefer something more intimate, and year-round? Head to Antiques Art & Collectibles near the Tip of the Mitt, where treasures await behind the colorful facade of adjoining 19th-century buildings. The owners have been hand-selecting beautiful pieces of the past since 1993 for collectors they call "History Keepers."

Allegan Antiques Market
150 Allegan County Fair Dr.,
Allegan, 269-673-6501
alleganantiques.com

Antiques Art & Collectibles
114 Stimpson St. (US-31 N),
Pellston, 231-539-8030
www.antiquesnorth.com

100

PICK UP A PIECE
OF PEWABIC POTTERY

A lasting contribution to the Arts and Crafts movement emerged from Detroit in the early 20th century. Pewabic Pottery grew out of a collaboration between Mary Chase Perry Stratton, a ceramic artist specializing in china painting, and Horace J. Caulkins, who invented the Revelation China Kiln that Mary favored. In 1903, they launched Pewabic, named after an Indian term for "clay with a copper color." Mary formulated unique iridescent metallic glazes for her architectural tiles, vases, and vessels in earthy colors with a warm, uneven, human touch.

The 1907 Pewabic Pottery building, a National Historic Landmark, is one of the country's oldest continuously operating potteries and is open for tours, special programs, workshops, and exhibitions. Its store carries many of Mary's original designs handcrafted by Pewabic artisans, like the graceful Snowdrop Vase in matte green and her iconic peacock art tile, as well as new pieces based on her signature colors and style. You'll also find the work of more than 30 independent ceramic artists.

10125 E Jefferson Ave., Detroit, 313-626-2000
pewabic.org

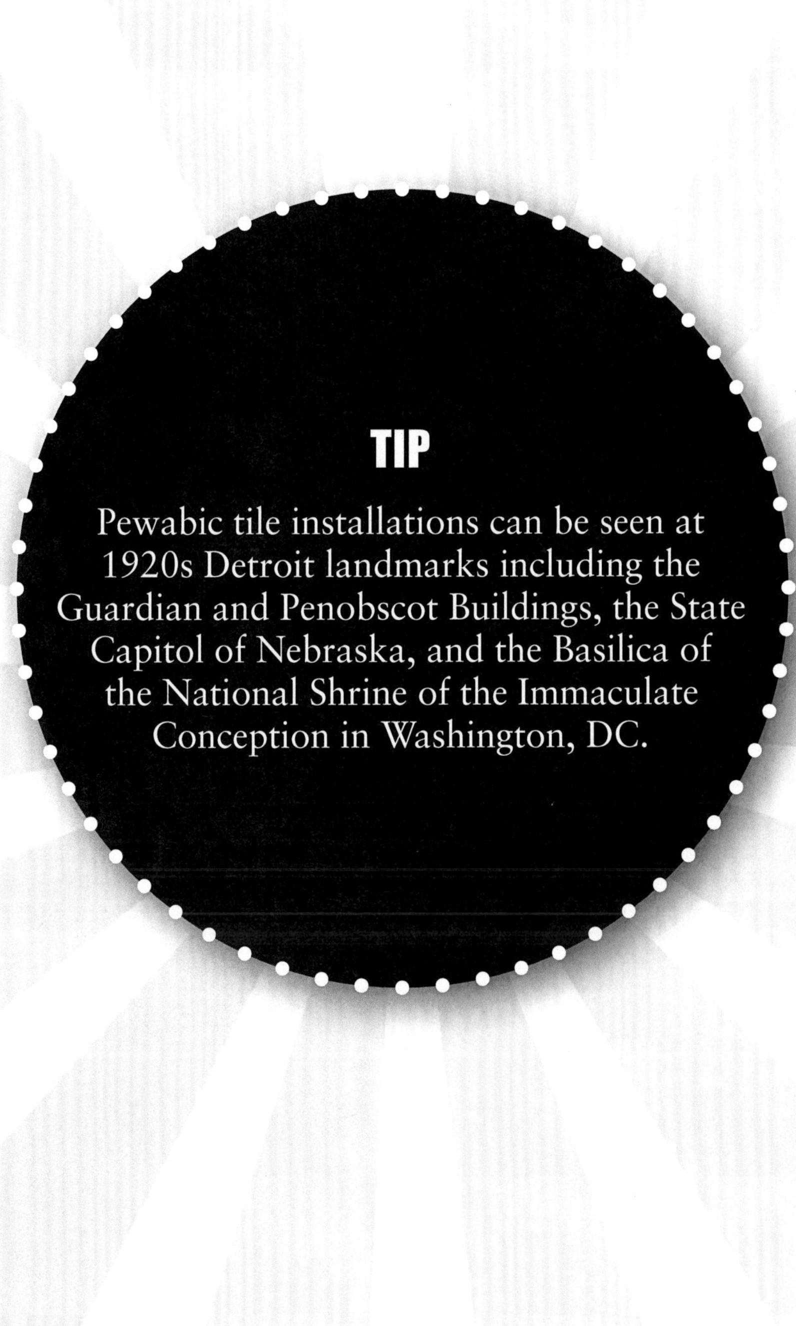

TIP

Pewabic tile installations can be seen at 1920s Detroit landmarks including the Guardian and Penobscot Buildings, the State Capitol of Nebraska, and the Basilica of the National Shrine of the Immaculate Conception in Washington, DC.

Ernest Hemingway, Walloon Lake

ACTIVITIES
BY SEASON

WINTER

SPRING

SUMMER

FALL

SUGGESTED ITINERARIES

FAMILY FUN

ESCAPE TO AN ISLAND

GET ARTSY

CULTURE KICKS

WATERY ADVENTURES

NATIONAL PARK IT

INDEX